MONEY
GROWS ON TREES

HOW TO RESHAPE YOUR THOUGHTS,

BELIEFS AND IDEALS ABOUT MONEY

AND BECOME TRULY WEALTHY

JERREMY
ALEXANDER
NEWSOME

ISBN-13: 978-1796451221

ISBN-10: 1796451223

Table of Contents

INTRODUCTION

I hope the next few pages you read sound outrageous and ostentatious. I want everything in this book to shake you to your very core! For years now it has been my deepest desire to become a world renowned *cerebral pyromaniac*! I have always wanted to create a literary work of art so mentally liberating and with such enriching content that the resulting book earns a permanent place on your bookshelf beside *Rich Dad Poor Dad, The Richest Man in Babylon, You Are a Badass at Making Money, MONEY: Master the Game, Killing Sacred Cows,* and of course *Money and the Meaning of Life.*

I truly believe I can be an inspiration and guide for you as you break free from your financial pressures. I *sincerely* trust that after you finish each and every word of this book, your beautiful brain will begin to impact you in such a profound way that the changes will be noticeable within weeks. Perhaps even hours!

It's important to note that almost nine years ago to the day of me writing this book, I had $0.01 in my bank account, which was super ironic - I mean, I actually *did* have a penny to my name, which by definition means I was massively broke. I'm sure you have heard that expression: "I'm so broke I don't even have a penny to my name." I mean, how poor is that exactly? It's obviously an exaggeration, because while I did have one penny to my name, I was still badly broke.

- I am talking about I knew the exact days and hours each grocery store had free samples, *broke*.

- I was at the stage where I would be friendly and super nice to people so I could eventually attend their weddings, graduation parties, birthday parties, business gatherings, Christmas parties and engagement parties so that I could eat the free food and drink the free drinks, *broke*.

- I was using the bathroom in public places, drinking only from water fountains, *broke*.

- Never applying sunscreen because it required money to purchase the sunscreen, *broke*.

- Wearing the same clothes for multiple days, *broke.*

- Only utilizing flip-flops so that I did not have to buy shoes and socks, *broke.*

- I was doing a single swipe on each arm to make the deodorant last longer, *broke.*

- Not having a bed frame or box spring and sleeping on just the mattress resting on the floor, *broke.*

- Clipping coupons, *broke.*

- Using BING instead of GOOGLE, *broke.*

- Using only the free version of Pandora, *broke.*

- Keeping my ex-girlfriend's Netflix sign in and using her account, *broke.*

- Taking my foot off the gas pedal and coasting down hills to "conserve gas," *broke.*

- Drinking Natural Light from a can, *broke.*

- Never buying or even reading free books, *broke.*

- Never investing in myself, *broke.*

The real problem is, I had no clue why I was *so broke*. I worked super hard. I knew math. I kind of knew that I needed to make more money than I spent, but somehow that was never the case. I felt as if I could *never* make more money than I needed to live, much less enough to live comfortably. I thought I had all the knowledge I needed to not be broke, but there I was, shopping at Kroger, listening to some music through my headphones (the ones that came with the phone) looking the cashier in her face while I was smiling, knowing my card was about to get declined. The entire time I was trying to wrangle up an excuse. I only had 4 items on the belt. Chicken breast, ramen noodles, a head of broccoli and one 16oz can of Fosters beer. Total, $7.89 - and I was about to NSF.

I swiped the card. The transaction went through. I was totally shocked, but 100% confident I was going to have a $35 NSF (non sufficient funds) fee hit my account that night, which meant that mathematically, this meal was about to cost $42.89.

Do you know what really hit me hard that night? Would you like to know the massive turning point? Let me tell you the story.

As I walked out of that Kroger around 11:57 pm, I found a penny on the ground. I leaned down, bag in my left hand, picked the penny up with my right hand and smiled. As I walked towards my car, I noticed this lady who appeared to be in massively dire straights. She shuffled towards me as she swayed through the barren, dimly lit parking lot. Her blonde hair looked like she'd ran a marathon in a hurricane, her grey sweat pants made it appear she'd just finished playing paint-ball in a ketchup factory, and her shoes were, well, they might be old Dasani bottles? I knew immediately she was going to ask for money. And I knew I had none.

As I got closer and closer to my 2010 silver Toyota Corolla, she too moved closer towards me. I was about 15 feet away from her and she asked loudly, "Sir, my car done broke down just a few miles down the road and I need gas money. Can I have some money for gas so I can get home to my four kids?"

I asked, "Where did your car break down?"

She pointed in a general direction.

"How much do you want?" I asked.

And she said, "Just some spare change?"

I said, "Ma'am, I appreciate you asking me, but I literally have *negative money* in my bank account. This bag contains all of my food for the next three days, I don't even know if I have enough gas to get home, and I'm truly the worst person you could ask for money - but I did find a penny about 15 seconds ago. Would that help?"

Her reply? "Well damn, it seems you might need the money more than I do." And she reached in her pocket and offered to give ME money! What???!! Are you kidding me? At this point I felt like collapsing! I had that weird feeling of wanting to run, cry, jump, yell, and laugh at the same time. My whole demeanor was massively confused.

I said to her, "Ma'am, thank you, but I can't accept your money. Here is the penny I found. I appreciate your generosity and I hope you find your way home." She smiled, accepted my penny, and walked towards the store. I honestly hope her life has worked out for the best, because that moment of generosity changed my life and set me down a path of introspection that could change the world.

Notice the word introspection. That very same night I began to think at length about why she had offered me money, but most importantly, why I'd turned it down. What if she *did* just run out of gas, but had millions in the bank? Was I *too good* for her money? Did I let my perception of how this lady looked, walked, and spoke create a judgment of her character?

Of course I judged her. I judged her hard! I took everything at face value. I didn't feel like she had any money, and I certainly didn't feel I deserved any of her money. So I started asking questions and talking to myself while I was sitting on the mattress that occupied my living room floor (since my house had no other furniture).

The questions I began to ask internally and even out loud (like a real crazy person) went something like this.

- Why am I so broke?

- How do I make more money?

- How hard do I have to work to make $100,000 a year?

- How do I make one million dollars?

And then I did something unique. I asked a question I had never asked anyone, especially myself.

I asked, "How much money do I deserve?"

And that question made my face bunch up. My body posture changed. It actually made me physically scratch my head, because I didn't have an answer to that question. When you don't have answers, what do you do?

You jump on the internet. In my case I used BING because they would "give a $0.10 credit for every one hour spent searching with them." And I searched, "How do I make more money." For the first time since high school, I started reading. And a few days later, I started reaching out to wealthy people. Over the next few days, weeks and months, I started asking different questions.

And my life changed forever.

> **"The quality of your questions determines the quality of your life." - Tony Robbins**

Let me help you do the same, right now. Let me list some questions that will shake you up a bit.

Questions like:

- Why are we told that money doesn't grow on trees?

- How did entire generations of people, *billions of humans*, grow up to believe that the love of money is evil?

- Why is the question "how much money do you make" so visceral and stabbing?

- Where did the term "filthy rich" come from?

- What do other cultures believe about money?

- Why do so many people believe the stock market is only moved by fear and greed?

- Is it true that rich people are mean, stuck up, and bossy?

- How much are you worth?

- How much do you want to be worth?

- How much money do you want?

- How much money do you feel you deserve?

If money was endless, how much would you have and what would you do with it?

The topics of money, sex, religion and politics are rarely discussed in the open, at least in a cohesive and uplifting way. That's my goal in the following pages. I want to tackle the mindset of money! I want both you and I to learn something together; to grow, progress, and enrich lives.

It's my objective in this literary journey to be the person that subliminally challenges you, while simultaneously changing many of your long held (usually subconscious) beliefs. This book, hopefully the first of many, is the culmination of my sleepless nights as 'ye olde brain' would not turn off as my mind constantly begged and prayed to *one day be successful*.

These ground breaking, life changing, and financially shifting words are the thoughts that I could no longer contain after a decade of thinking differently, asking insanely good questions, observing, listening, studying, reaching out, volunteering, giving, crying, hugging, writing, deliberating and waiting.

"The two most important days in your life are the day you are born and the day you find out why."

Well, Mr. Mark Twain, I am very happy you found your why. And I am also very thankful to have stumbled across mine as well. My mission and my why is **to enrich lives through mentally liberating education**. *Your* mission right now is to finish this entire book. In my life, I've found it super easy to start something; however, it's always much harder to finish. Determination, perseverance, and discipline are important personal attributes to success, but it's our actual beliefs that will either hold us back from starting, or prevent us from finishing.

So far, you are doing incredible! Keep reading and let's enrich lives together, because at the end of this book, your life will never be the same. After you finish this book you will have completed one more step on your marathon of becoming wealthy! And I am talking about *real financial riches*.

I am talking living life to your fullest potential, *wealthy*!

Like making $10,000 a month while you sleep, *wealthy*!

Looking at your multiple bookshelves with hundreds of books that you've read cover-to-cover, *wealthy*.

Affording personal chefs, *wealthy*.

Driving whatever cars and flying in whatever planes you want, *wealthy*.

Owning 100,000 shares of AAPL, *wealthy*.

Actually having multiple lock boxes at multiple banks, *wealthy*.

Never needing a bank for money, because you are your own bank, *wealthy*!

Having multiple businesses, *wealthy*.

Going to whatever restaurant you want, *wealthy*.

Tipping the waiter 100% and smiling about it, *wealthy*.

Having the most stable, kind, warm, welcoming relationship with your family, *wealthy*.

Sleeping in as long as you want, *wealthy*.

Flying first class to Rome with your entire family on a Tuesday because it's exciting, *wealthy*!

Feeding millions of homeless people each year, *wealthy*!

Being 100% financially free, *wealthy*.

Having your own foundations, *wealthy*.

Affording the best healthcare on the planet, *wealthy*.

Building schools and hospitals and centers of learning, because you want to improve your community, *wealthy*.

Finding your WHY and living it every day, *wealthy*!

My friend, thank you for taking this journey with me. We are on it together and I'm right beside you, each step of the way. Let us contribute, grow, love, progress, help others, and discover how incredible you are when you have unlimited resources at your disposal!

CHAPTER ONE:
Money Does Grow On Trees

There I was, hands stained purple, standing in front of her screen door at 7 years of age. I was wearing tattered, mud stained jean shorts (yep, jorts), totally shoeless and shirtless, eyes filled with determination and unbridled optimism. In my left hand was a zip lock bag that I 'borrowed' from the top drawer of my kitchen next to the refrigerator.

Inside the bag were probably 50 hand picked blackberries. My goal was to sell these blackberries in exchange for US currency. My unpolished, unscripted sales pitch went something like this. "Good afternoon, Ma'am! My name is Jerremy Alexander Newsome, and today is your lucky day. That's because just hours ago, I hand picked these blackberries just for you and I would love to give them to you for only $1.00."

Honestly, looking back now, even after 20 years of sales experience, that was one crisp delivery. But what I really had going for me (other than the jorts) was my age. Let's think about it. What do you think the closing rate is of a shirtless 7 year old, standing on your porch selling blackberries for 70% less than what they cost in an actual store? The only way my closing rate would have been higher is if *every single person* was home when I knocked on the door. If I spoke with you, you had yourself a bag of blackberries. That summer, back in 1995, I made roughly $1,300 selling blackberries. Why is this important? What groundbreaking and revolutionary impact does this story have? Time to dive in.

It was only a few weeks prior I watched the movie *Forrest Gump* for the first time. Do you remember towards the end, when Forrest is recounting his life experiences, you see him walking up to a mailbox where he says, "Lieutenant Dan invested us in a fruit company. And he said we didn't have to worry about money any more. I thought, great, one less thing to worry about."

I was sitting on our beige couch. To the left of me was my oldest brother, Jerry-Roger, and to his left was our dad. I asked, "Dad, what is investing?" He gave me his fatherly answer and then I said, "What is the fruit company?" Where he then told me about Apple Computers.

After his semi lengthy reply about Apple Computers, I said forcefully, "Dad, you should do what Forrest did and invest in Apple Computers."

To which he replied, "Son, it's not that simple. This is a movie. Things aren't real in movies. It doesn't work that way. Money just doesn't grow on trees. I can't just *invest* into Apple Computers."

After that specific moment, I had only one dream: to never worry about money anymore. It seemed that was always the topic of discussion in my house - how there was never enough money to do well, anything, really. If it was free or cheap, we could do it. Otherwise, there was a strong chance of it *not* happening.

Several weeks later, I finally convinced my dad later to buy shares of Apple. He said, "Son, I'll make you a deal. If you give me the money to invest, I'll match dollar for dollar whatever you bring to me." And, my friend, that was my spark. That was my fire! It was fully lit, and I was prepared to do anything I could to bring my dad money so we could invest and then no longer worry about money anymore. Just like Forrest.

I had very limited resources at the time. My question then was and is the question many find themselves asking on a daily basis. "How do I get money?" I asked this question over and over. One random day as I was walking down Macedonia Road, which to this day is still a dirt road, I was hungry and bored; so I stopped and picked some blackberries. As I was walking home popping some into my mouth, I thought, *"These are great. I'm sure other people probably like blackberries. I'll just pick them and sell them door to door!"*

You might laugh when I say this, but I didn't realize the significance of that moment until a few months ago, and ever since that light bulb moment, I've been planning on creating this very book along with the Money Grows on Trees live events! Speaking of, make sure you visit the live event website treesaremoney.com and find out the details of the next live event!

My entire life, I have heard people say "Money doesn't grow on trees." I mean, this is just a common phase. Over the span of my life I have heard it from from presidents to mentors, bosses to business owners, friends, family, gas station clerks, bar tenders, professors, bankers, market makers, Uber drivers, taxi drivers, pilots you get the picture.

Only mere months ago did I realize how untrue this statement was, and it occurred in a conversation I had with one of my clients. I was working with a gentleman on his finances. He was not where he wanted to be financially. In fact, the polar opposite. He was in over $20,000 of debt. He hated his job, his marriage was on the rocks, and he needed my help trading the stock market to *finally* make some money and break free from his financial chains.

Obviously, you and I both know it wasn't 'stock market' advice he needed. We proceeded to chat about how he could make more money. I brought up things he could do, items he could sell, jobs he could apply for, bills he needed to focus on and at some point in the conversation, he literally said, "Yeah man, that's great and all, I would love to pay that credit card off, but money doesn't just grow on trees."

And my reply was incredible! It was almost like I had scripted it. But I actually had never had this thought before. I had never uttered these words aloud, nor thought them in silence.

I said to him, "Oh, but it *does*!"

His face resembled that look someone has when you slap them a little too hard on their sunburned back.

The next few sentences and paragraphs are so revolutionary and original, you might be tempted to shut the book and immediately look for someone to tell this newly found secret. You are about to learn, for a fact, that everything you believe about money is wrong. We are taught our whole lives that money doesn't grow on trees. Meaning, we can't just open our door, walk outside, and pick money off of a tree to go spend it on what we want, need, or crave.

But that's exactly what I did as a child! I went and picked something off of a bush and exchanged it for money.

Ponder this: What is an apple? You would agree, I'm sure, that it is a fruit. At your local market, if you want that apple, what is required? Some of your money, right? The farmers who plant apple orchards do it because those delicious morsels are worth money so if you are an apple farmer, money literally grows on trees.

And it doesn't stop there. Pears, oranges, bananas, coconuts, mangos, avocados, peaches, limes, lemons, cherries, walnuts, pecans, pistachios shoot! All of them grow on trees, don't they?

Then you have things that grow on vines! Grapes, watermelons, squash, eggplant, peas, cantaloupes, honeydew and pumpkins. You have to pay money for all of those as well.

Another example would be maple syrup! It doesn't even grow on a tree, but comes from *inside* of the tree.

Does this make sense? All of these things can be planted, grown, cultivated and exchanged for money! This line of thinking will help you shift your definition of money. Two hundred years ago, the money you currently use would be worthless. No one would know what it is or what it means. And 200 years from now, the money you presently use will be obsolete and probably no longer in circulation.

Money is just a way to measure exchange and utilization. That's all money is. Money is a tool. Money can be anything. It can look like anything. It all comes down to our perception of what's important and what's useful. Money is a tool of representation!

> **"Money can be a brick to build a home or a brick to throw through a window." ~ Dave Ramsey**

It can be an apple or an orange. It can be a dollar or a euro. It can be gold or silver. It can be seashells or sticks of wood. What I realized is that money means whatever we want it to mean. We have the ability to place or remove meaning. To craft importance or remove it. To use the money tool for useful exchanges, selfish exchanges, kind and loving exchanges, or devious exchanges.

Our thoughts control our lives. Our beliefs control our lives! And if we can see these facts, if we can understand the truth that money is never the problem, that idea will cause a monumentally massive shift in our life! If people were taught that money is everywhere and that they simply have to find it, how impactful would that be?

I can think of so many arguments my parents had over money. And we could all agree that many marriages or long held relationships end in a divorce over some financial issues and constraints. If people knew that money does grow on trees, that mental barrier could be removed forever. What excuse would they then have? If money freely grows on trees, then money is a resource. Which implies that *everyone always has the ability to get more money.*

Let's say you need $40,000. I'm sure everyone reading this would love an extra $40,000.

So Jerremy, how do I go about walking outside and plucking $40,000 from a tree?

Go rob a bank.

Kidding! I'm kidding - don't do that. I mean, it *is* a way to get $40,000, but it is a really stupid, negative and maniacal way to obtain it. You should never steal money from others to get the money you want. Why? Because there is so much money to go around. There is no need to steal, just go make it.

Here is a question. Let's say you have a job at a company. If you could find a way for your company to obtain 40,000 brand new customers, would you receive some benefit for that?

Absolutely yes! Of course you would! Shoot, if you bring ME 40,000 new customers, I'll ensure you receive a massive benefit for that.

Or what about my self-employed folks? If you got

40,000 new clients, customers or purchases would you then likely receive an extra $40,000 to your bottom line? Most likely, the answer is yes. In fact, you probably couldn't handle an extra 40,000 people showing up to your door, store, cash register, show room or email inbox. But you get the point. Which means we should not ask, "How do we get $40,000," because it's there. We have to find it. We simply need to find which tree it's growing on.

We have to believe the truth that money is everywhere! There is an endless amount of money. There is just no end to the vastness of money. More will always and can always be created.

Do you know how much money is out there in the world? There are enough US Dollars alone for every single person on this earth to have $1,000,000,000. Yep, that's 1 billion dollars. Every human on this planet just joined the triple comma club. If we want $40,000, or $400,000, or $40,000,000, we simply have to become resourceful enough to create that much value!

I believe it was Zig Ziglar who once said, "If you want to make $1,000,000, solve a problem for 1,000,000 people."

I've learned in my life that it's not the lack of resources, but one's lack of *resourcefulness* that holds us back from achieving what we want. What does that mean exactly?

Money is not the issue. There is plenty of money for YOU. If you want to create your very own business, write a book, travel to Fiji, donate, give, help, provide, tip, all of the money you want, all of the money you deserve, is out there. It's our beliefs about money that hold us back. And here we have already conquered and overcome one of the biggest lies about money that exists.

How many more false beliefs are out there?

How many more lies about money do you subconsciously believe?

Which falsehoods hold you back the most, without you even knowing it?

Many of these beliefs, statements, phrases and idioms might never consciously enter our thoughts, yet they are still buried deep in your mind. Every second, minute and hour of each day your subconscious mind mulls over certain topics without your knowledge. It even feels certain things without your knowledge.

You must understand that *your subconscious beliefs about money* is what led you to the exact financial situation you find yourself in right now.

That might sound crazy, but it's 100% true. Whether you are making $34,000, $78,000, $126,000, $254,230, or $1,400,405 a year, it's because you believed something specific. You have independent thoughts, actions and beliefs that caused you to make that amount. Your mind contains everything you need to make as much money as you feel you deserve. Let me show you one more quick example. I would love to blow your mind just once more in this chapter. What is most money made out of? Paper, right? And where do we get paper? FROM TREES!

Meaning, TREES ARE MONEY! *Hand motion signifying a brain explosion*

Not only does money grows on trees, but trees in themselves are actually money.

Paper bills were first used by the Chinese, who started carrying folding money during the Tang Dynasty (A.D. 618-907) — mostly in the form of privately issued bills of credit or exchange notes — and used it for more than 500 years before the practice began to catch on in Europe in the 17th century.

At its root, all of this means that most people in the world, *billions* of people, walk around all day believing something that is morally, factually and literally incorrect. Money DOES grow on trees.

I want you to really think about how this one singular mind shift can and will impact your life! It's the mindset of abundance. It frees your subconscious mind to actually believe, finally *believe*, that money is everywhere.

27

Will you continue reading this book to discover what other thoughts, ideas and learned beliefs might be holding you back? I mean, if you have to close this book now and go tell everyone near you that money grows on trees and they can have as much money as they feel they deserve, I understand. I'll be right here in the next chapter waiting for you!

As mentioned previously, I would love for you to visit treesaremoney.com and check out everything that's offered there! What a great website name, right?

Some notes for you to write down! Believe them, because they are true.

Money is abundant.

Money is everywhere, it even grows on trees!

It's not your lack of money holding you back.

To get more money, which is a resource, simply become more resourceful.

My challenge to you to accomplish in the next 10 minutes:

Ask someone, "Have you ever heard the phrase, money doesn't grow on trees?" and see how well you can explain the concept that it DOES!

CHAPTER TWO:
The Love Of Money Is
The Root Of All Evil?

First Timothy 6:10 - "For the love of money is the root of all evil."

Defining love is interesting. I hit up my buddy Webster for this one. The definition found there is short and sweet: "An intense feeling of deep affection."

Let me give this definition a shot as well. If someone loves another person, that individual probably thinks about the other person a lot. That person is always on their mind, always wanting to be around that person, wanting more time with that person, telling other people about that person, and visualizing a future with that person. Bottom line, that person consumes a high percentage of their mental processes. It would then seem that they love that person.

This was an interesting concept for me to tackle in my mind. Until recently, I always believed there was nobility in being poor, broke and penniless. I always believed being in that financial situation showed others I was humble, hungry, and it showed that I was willing to work hard to make money, a real salt of the earth type. I never even questioned the above belief until one of my dear friends who lives in Canada uttered the following words in a phone conversation we had.

She said, "I never made *a lot* of money until I simply accepted the fact that I loved money." This took me by surprise as this particular person was (and is) very loving, giving, generous and philanthropic. This person is always gifting, helping, donating, attending charity functions, and volunteering, and her family unit is one I would consider to be warm and cherished.

Cumulatively I've spent weeks with this person, so that particular statement really shook me. Is my friend 'evil?' She just admitted out loud that she loves money. Who in their right mind would love money? Wouldn't that inherently make that person evil and greedy? And therein lies a true issue for billions of people here on Earth. We have all failed to really dissect that statement.

"For the love of money is the *root* of all evil." This does not mean if you love money you are evil. It does not say love of money will automatically make you a bad person. My friend, if we go back to my tree analogy, we get to determine how our tree grows, and it all starts from the roots! We get to decide what type of fruit our tree produces, how much fruit it produces, who uses our fruit, how often they use it, and why. We get to determine what grows from our root system, and how much grows. We get to choose how much we keep, and how much we provide for others.

The biggest challenge here for most readers is likely that they do love money. But for their entire lives, they have been afraid to admit it! Why? Because no one wants to be evil.

Do you remember learning about the transitive property? If A=B and B=C, then A=C. That's one of the few things I ever learned in math class, and it applies beautifully in this example. I would argue that most people think about money very frequently. It's something that pops into their head daily. They want more money. They want to be around money more often. They tell others all the glorious things they would do with money. They dream about all the experiences they would have and trips they would take if they had more money.

Countless people lie awake at night wanting to provide

abundantly for their family and others. Billions of us are consumed with how much money we would donate, the countless people we would help, and all the roads, hospitals, schools and businesses we'd build if only we had *more money*. In essence, people love money. But if they (A) *love money*, and (B), the love of money is *the root of all evil*, then (C) *you are the root of all evil*, because you (A) *love money*.

Since no one wants to be inherently evil, they simply tell themselves, "*I do not love money. I refuse to believe it.*" If you tell yourself, **"I do not love money because I do not want to be evil" How much money do you think will ever come into your life?**

Perhaps deep in your subconscious mind you always push money away simply because you do not want to be evil. How will you ever become as rich as you truly want, desire, and deserve if you are always pushing money away?

Consciously you already know how exciting it would be to have money! I mean, heck, you think about having more money and wanting more money every single day - likely every waking hour! But since your moral beliefs and subconscious thoughts are always saying '*you are the root of all evil since you love money*', it has become insanely difficult to get more! This is the result of having these two opposing forces.

It's like one person is turning on water, and another person is standing next to them and immediately turning the water off. How much water will flow out if that is what's continuously occurring? Think of how confusing that is! One part of you (the stronger part) doesn't want to love money because it *'makes you evil,'* yet another part of you craves and loves money. It's a seesaw effect that produces no direction. It's due to a long-held belief that you have always been scared to admit.

It's okay to love money because YOU are not evil. My friend, your roots have already grown! Your tree is already planted! Now we need to water it, fertilize it, cultivate it, and harvest its bounty.

You have probably heard the saying that money only exemplifies who you *already are.* Money only amplifies how *you* feel, think and act. Are there wealthy people who are evil? Yes. Are there poor people who are evil? Yes. There are evil people that come in every color, sex, shape and size.

The good news is that the percentages are extremely small! For every insanely rich person who also happens to be a giant turd face, you'll find 100 insanely wealthy people that are the most loving, kind, giving, and generous souls in the world. You just haven't heard of them, because many prefer to remain anonymous in their giving and donations. I'll give you an example.

Have you ever heard of Chuck Feeney?

Charles Francis "Chuck" Feeney was born April 23, 1931. He is an Irish-American businessman and philanthropist, and the founder of The Atlantic Philanthropies one of the largest private foundations in the world. He made his fortune as a co-founder of the Duty Free Shoppers Group, which pioneered the concept of duty-free shopping. This amazing soul gave away his fortune in secret for many years, until a business dispute resulted in his identity being revealed in 1997. Over the course of his life, he has given away more than $8 billion US Dollars! And that's just one small instance. There are myriads of examples just like that of Chuck Feeney.

One could easily make the argument that if you are poor, your brain is pre-wired to find only the mean and greedy rich people. If you *already* think that's how rich people act, do you think your brain wants you to be wealthy? No chance.

Many people envision rich and wealthy people as stuck up, mean, snooty, uncouth and uncool hippos, rife with judgments with snarky faces and sneering eyes. As it turns out, if you believe in something, that's all you'll see. Where thoughts go, energy will flow.

I bet if you challenged yourself right now though, you would be unable to write down the first and last name of just ten rich people who are horrific, mean, greedy, miserly, and who hate puppies and family gatherings.

Go ahead. Try and think of 10 and write their names down:

1.

2.

3.

4.

5.

6.

7.

8.

9.

10.

Now sure, you might get through four or five, but did you really come up with 10? Also, make sure you know these people personally. Not just people you have seen on TV or the news. Unless you interact with them on a daily basis, you have no idea how they actually are.

Sure, we are all know there are a lot of pompous, mean, arrogant, flamingo hating, endangered animal poaching, racist bigots out there. Tons of those people. But most of those people are not wealthy! Many of them will not have gobs of money.

Here's an often-cited statistic for you. *The world's wealthiest individuals, those owning over $100,000 in assets, total only 8.6 % of the global population but own 85.6 % of global wealth.*

So, 8.6% of the humans on this planet have 85.6% of the wealth. Is that because they are smarter than you? Meaner than you? Luckier than you? Born with it? Inherited it? Why are they so rich?!

It's because of their beliefs!

We know without a doubt that there are certainly tens of thousands of individuals on this planet who love money *and* are the epitome of evil. Their roots were fed with greed, hatred, and a system of beliefs that thrive on exclusion. Yet there are tens of millions of wonderful, cheerful, happy, spiritual, joyous, curious, realistic, and wealthy individuals on this planet. Hopefully, one day, there will be billions in this situation!

When is the last time you walked into a huge zoo - like a national zoo?

Three months ago, I was at the San Diego Zoo and do you know what I noticed? Dozens of plaques, recognizing the charitable donations of certain people, reaching tens of thousands of dollars a piece if not more. I mean, entire exhibits were sponsored and made possible thanks to these generous gifts from kind people. Six months ago I was in Denver, Colorado touring the Art Museum downtown. Again, loads of plaques, memorials, statues, funds, exhibits, hallways, water fountains, and gift shops were all made possible through people's gifts and donations.

Just sit down and think for a minute about all of the good that money does for others and know in your heart, that if you openly accept your love of money, it will flow towards you! It can finally give you the opportunity to bestow rich blessings on so many others as you have always wanted to do.

My advice? Start right now! There's no need to wait.

Vernor Vinge said, "Even the largest avalanche is triggered by small things."

Matt Bevin was quoted saying, "While it may seem small, the ripple effects of small things is extraordinary."

What does this mean? If you want to give to others, if you want to help others, if you want to grow and think in abundance, start doing it now! It might seem small to you, but it can be large to others. Do not wait until you have $1,000,000 before you give $100 in cash as a tip for a $20 meal. Do not wait until you have $10,000,000 before you pay for the family's meal beside you. Grow and water the roots of your money tree now! If you want to be a loving, generous, thoughtful human being, you must start at this exact moment in time!

If you want to tip at 30% when you are rich, start tipping 30% right now. Remember, money will only exemplify who you are on the inside. It will make your thoughts brighter, your voice louder, your plans more impactful, and your ideas more concrete!

Here are the points for you to write down. Believe them, because they are true. Say these phrases out loud and in your mind every day!

I love money and money loves me!

I love money because of all the incredible things I can accomplish with its help!

I sincerely love money, because it will amplify who I already am, and I'm an amazing human!

I truly love money, and I will use it to bless and help vast numbers of people!

Money is everywhere, it even grows on trees. In fact, trees are money!

My challenge for you to accomplish within the next seven days:

The next item that you pay for that has a tip line, either:

Ask: "if I put a tip on here, will it go to you?" and if the answer is yes, tip them 50% of whatever the bill was. No question.

If the answer is no, give them cash if you have it handy. If you do not have any cash, go get some and be prepared to give it to the next person!

CHAPTER THREE:
Are You Greedy,
Because You Say It A Lot?

This one is exciting! You are going to have so many breakthroughs and mind revelations in this chapter, you should probably buy a fire extinguisher - because I'm about to light up that brain!

First, a super quick back story:

Many of you may know that I've been heavily involved in the stock market since I was 20 years old. As I write this, it has been a tad longer than a decade. One thing that always struck a nerve with me was people calling me 'greedy' because I wanted to make money in the stock market. In fact, the whole premise of the market is said to be driven by fear and greed.

Is there greed in the stock market? Of course! Shoot, there is greed in the super market down the road! But is that the driving force? Are the markets actually driven by *greed*? Is the vast majority that participates truly greedy? Are *you* greedy?

Hell no! You're a massive optimist! I can't emphasize enough that the words, thoughts and beliefs you use each day will shape your life. This notion is extremely similar to the previous chapter. Yet, upon further inspection, you'll see that it's an entirely separate deal. We're about to look at a totally different subconscious barrier that we need to unblock so you can become wealthy.

About eight years ago when I was really *just* diving into the stock market in earnest, one of my friends at the time asked me a question. He asked, "How much money do you want to make per year doing this?" My reply was, "Oh, I just want to make enough to live on, man. Enough to quit my job would be great!" And he said, "How much is that?" To which I replied, "Oh, like $60,000 a year would be great!" He replied, "$60,000? Dang man, I thought you were going to say like $2,000,000 or something." I laughed, then scoffed, uttered a weird sound, and said, "Dude, I don't need that much, man. I don't want to be *greedy*."

Ironically, I didn't even think about this conversation, my reply, his perception of my skills, *or any of it* until just a couple of years ago. In the incredible book *You Are A Badass at Making Money* by Jen Sincero, she recommends that you think about a time when you felt judged about how much money you were or were not making. That moment I just described was one of many that popped into my head after some thought.

This was and still is one of my core values and beliefs, *I am not greedy*. I am a generous, joyous, humble, caring, creative, thoughtful, and devoted guy! I love milkshakes so much! I also love *money* so much. It's the same love! Why am I allowed to openly love milk-shakes, which have such limited resources, power, and scope, yet if I love money, I'm labeled greedy?

Why should I think I am greedy because I want more money? What's wrong with more money? Isn't that what I want in the first place? Will more money *make* me greedy? If so, how much more money would make me greedy? $10? $100,000?

Here's the kicker my friend, another ultimate truth. If you have a number, *any* number, ANY figure in your head that says "I'm greedy if I have this much money," then it's going to be *very hard* for you to achieve financial riches. You are making it almost impossible on yourself. Why?

Because with every single dollar you earn, you get closer to the "I'm greedy" mark. And *no one* wants to be greedy! So with every dollar you gain, you find yourself heading towards a path that you **do not** want to head towards. This causes your mind and even your body to always turn away from money. Again, another dichotomy. Two opposing forces.

To break through this impasse, we must remember that greed is just a state of the soul! Being greedy means that you can never have enough, you can never be quenched, you can never be satisfied, and you want it all for yourself. My friend, *let's find out if you're greedy*.

- If at any point in your life you saw an abandoned child, a homeless person, someone who obviously needed help AND YOU HELPED THEM, you are not greedy.

- If at any point in your life you wanted more money to enrich the lives of your family, friends and loved ones, you are not greedy.

- If you were moved to tears of joy when you received a $20 bill as a gift from your grandma at Christmas, you are not greedy.

- If at any point in your life you became super excited about a bonus at work, knowing you'd be able to give more to your favorite religious organization, charity, or foundation, you are not greedy.

- If in the past you had a friend forget their wallet and you paid for their burger, and neither expected nor wanted to be repaid, you are not greedy.

- If you have dined with friends or family and picked up the whole check as a sign of appreciation and affection, you are not greedy.

- If you regularly give gifts or presents, especially hand made ones, you are not greedy.

- If you are generally accepted by your friends, co-workers, and peers as a nice person, you probably are not greedy as greedy people generally don't have many friends.

- If you loved hugs from your grandparents, you probably are not greedy.

Bottom line, if you do anything for anyone else at any time, by definition, you are not greedy.

So there you go, I give you full permission to love money and want more money! There is plenty for everyone! If you, *yes you*, took ALL OF THE MONEY in the world - every single piece of gold, silver, dollar, yuan, euro, bitcoin, peso and dinar, there's a 100%

chance you would just be spreading that back to others.

- You would build stuff, which would cost money.

- You would buy stuff, which would cost money.

- You would hire people, which would cost money.

- And you would probably give most of it away.

And even if you didn't - even if you did hoard every last fragment of both value and monies, us "outsiders" would just go create a new form of currency, and boom, there would be more money again. **Money isn't a thing, it's just an idea! If you want more ideas, you have to think different thoughts.**

Boom! Game changer, right? This book could be 200 pages long with nothing else written on the pages except for that quote, and it would be worth it.

Most people internally struggle with how their family, friends, co-workers and others would **judge them** if they became wealthy. One of the things that held me back subconsciously for years was the idea of being viewed differently by my family. I created a false narrative and an incorrect perception on how my family would feel towards me if I got money.

I conjured up ideas that I would walk into a room on Thanksgiving and everyone would say, "Oh, there's

Mr. Moneybags." This *story* that I built into my own mind was a cage keeping me from wealth. I didn't want anyone to ever think I was greedy, and I thought having lots of money and loving money was the same as greed. I was also mortified of the possibility that someone in my family would ask me for money, knowing I would probably say no. This could then cause them to say, "Oh, you want to hoard all the money for yourself, because you're just greedy."

What's interesting is none of the above scenarios ever happened. I have been asked for money from my family, and I did say no, but I was not called greedy, at least, not yet. However, at this point, even if I were called greedy, it would not bother me. I now know it's simply untrue.

That's where another insanely powerful quote comes in. In her book *A Return To Love: Reflections on the Principles of A Course in Miracles* by Marianne Williamson, she wrote a poem called *Our Deepest Fear*. This poem is epic, so go read it, but I'd like to dissect the following lines:

> Our deepest fear is not that we are inadequate.

> Our deepest fear is that we are powerful beyond measure.

Let me break that down for a few moments. This is going to be a huge point, so if you are tired, distracted, or hungry - anything other than totally enthralled and in the zone, get in a good stretch, shake up that body, and let's continue.

One more time - "Our deepest fear is not that we are inadequate. Our deepest fear is that we are powerful beyond measure."

The struggle many people will have in this world, the same one I battled with, is becoming ashamed of leaving who we once were to become who we need to be. As humans, many of us know and embrace comfort. We are okay with our current lifestyle, friends, job, and surroundings. We are content with our finances, relationships, emotional fortitude, and spirituality. Changing any of them will be painful or uncomfortable.

Many of us know what failure looks like and feels like. If I asked you, what does ultimate failure look like? You might say, 'well, I lose my job somehow, my spouse leaves me, my kids resent me, and I have no money.'

Let's say two of those things occur. Let us pretend you lost your job right now and then all of the money you have, every dime, somehow just vanished from all your accounts. Your stock holdings, savings, *everything*. If you have money in a safe, that's gone too. You can't pay your mortgage or your rent, then what happens? Your family has to live somewhere, right? Where can you go?

The answer is probably shocking. You likely have a friend or family member who would welcome you with open arms if something tragic like that occurred. Granted, it's certainly not *best case scenario*, and you likely would not be irrevocably happy, yet you would have a place to stay and food to eat.

Then again, even if you had nothing, no friends nor family to assist you, no money, no religious congregation members to assist, no previous co-workers, zero help of any kind, where could you go? You're probably conjuring up images of you and your family at a homeless shelter right now, but the truth is, if it comes down to it, at least you have a place to stay for a few nights until you become resourceful enough to find or think of *someone* to help you. You could find a job and start clawing your way back. But often times, worse case scenario is not that bad. I've been there.

I wasn't at homeless-with-a-drug-addition rock bottom. I was able to maintain my job and housing, but as described in the introduction to this book, I definitely reached some very low spots in my early 20s. The irony in all of this worrying we do is **most of us already know what worst case scenario is**. We have thought about it. We have dreamed about it, talked about it, and feared it. We have stayed in the jobs we hated to avoid it.

As humans, we are already programmed to fear the

unknown. We also *know* what failure is, and even though we *think* we fear it, we really don't. We just don't want to be there. We don't want to indulge failure and live in a world of worst case scenario because we think it would be painful and joyless.

So, because we fear the unknown and dare not step into it, almost no one ever lives to their fullest potential. We assume that the unknown is a non-compelling and scary future. Since we've already assumed that the unknown is dangerous, we subconsciously group the unknown with the worst-case scenarios we're constantly thinking about.

Here's a question for you - **what is the best case scenario?**

Most humans have *no clue* what best case scenario could be. They do not believe it's possible, much less have they given any serious time to think about, ponder over, daydream, or physically write down their best case scenario. Yet this is something we did often when we were young, right? The "what do you want to be when you grow up" question. Some might answer astronaut, professional sports player, race car driver, super hero, laser shooting ninja. Those vast dreams die when the complexities, pressures, and money barriers enter our lives as teenagers and then adults.

But why?

It all boils down to our beliefs. If you created your best case scenario, would you believe it's possible? Would you write down steps of how it's achievable? For example, imagine if you simply physically wrote down the statement "I want to have $14,000,000 in liquid cash in my bank account within the next five years." That would be a HUGE step! Even just having one big goal at least pulls you towards it.

Now we have to figure out which tree has that money. What are you going to create, build, achieve or solve to receive that amount of money? If money is an idea, which idea can you craft to ensure your dream becomes a reality? Can you sell something? Can you create something? Write something? Building something? Find something? Which problem can you solve? Where can you create massive value?

We know for sure the $14,000,000 is out there waiting for you. The question then simply becomes 'how do I become valuable enough to deserve that amount of money?'

First: You have to sincerely believe there is enough money out there for you to have $14,000,000, knowing you didn't take it away from someone.

Second: You simply have to build a realistic path towards that goal. This is where most successful people begin to focus their talents and skills to provide massive value to myriads of people. Here are some examples of ways you could have obtained that $14,000,000.

You could have 14,000,000 million people give you $1.

You could have sold 395 homes worth $1,300,000 and receive 3% commission for each sale. 3% of $1,300,000 = $39,000. And $39,000 x 395 = $15,405,000 in sales commissions. True story! And that is just one sale per week for a 7.5 years.

Perhaps you wrote a best selling book, receiving 10% of sales (about $1.48 per book), meaning only 9,459,459 people need to buy the book! It's possible, right?!

- Maybe you created, produced, or worked on a multiplatinum album?

- You could have built and amassed 14,000,000 followers on social media.

- Did you help your company generate $1.4 billion dollars in revenue?

- Did you and your team uncover a sunken ship full of gold?

- Did you write all of the words for a number one hit single?

- Were you the leading role in a feature film?

- Did you create, build, or help create an e-commerce website that sells really epic sunglasses to millions of people annually where you get a percentage of sales or some cut of the revenue?

Once you determine your goal, come up with a way to achieve that goal which involves your talent(s) and expertise! Everyone has talent of some kind. Everyone has skills of some kind. It can be gardening, painting, taking care of special needs children, cooking, writing, running, or swimming. With the internet and technology where it's at the present moment, and where it's going in the future, everyone in the world will have the access and capability to create value for others, thus creating value for themselves!

It's imperative to really think about **best case scenario** in your life. As Tony Robbins says "It's better to be led by your dreams than pushed by your problems."

My challenge for you to accomplish within the next seven days:

> **Begin to craft your best case scenario! Share it with people in your family. Have them do the exercise as well.**
>
> **Write out in detail what you would do on every given day of the week if you have $14,000,000 of cash in your bank account.**

What would you do with the money? How would you keep it, and better yet, grow it? What investments would you make? Which books would you read? What would your daily schedule look like?

Really put yourself into that world and think about how amazing that would be. Free of guilt, free of greed, financial abundance surrounding you.

Remember to say these words everyday:

I love money and money loves me!

I love money because of all the incredible things I can accomplish with its help!

I sincerely love money because it will amplify who I already am, and I'm an amazing human!

I truly love money, and I will use it to bless and help vast numbers of people!

Money is everywhere, it even grows on trees. In fact, trees are money!

CHAPTER FOUR:
How Much Do You Deserve?

I was so excited to reach and write this chapter because I feel this subject is overlooked and neglected. Remember, the ability for you to *actually* achieve your goals comes from your beliefs before your actions. Even if you do the proper actions, take the accurate steps, attend the correct seminars, and read the right books, it can all vanish and crumble without the proper belief system. In short, it's not what you know, but what you believe which can lead to lasting change! The fun part for me is that this subject can easily put people on edge.

Brian Tracy said, "Move out of your comfort zone. You can only grow if you are willing to feel awkward and uncomfortable when you try something new."

Well, we are here. Let's be okay with feeling 'awk-ward' for just a few minutes while you read this. This is likely the first time you have ever worked with, dealt with, heard of, or thought through this process. I'll come out and say people do deserve certain things, right? There are basic needs and elements which humans both need and deserve to have in order to live. Love, being one of those needs.

Someone once said, "You can search throughout the entire universe for someone who is more deserving of your love and affection than you are yourself, and that person is not to be found anywhere. You yourself, as much as anybody in the entire universe, deserve your love and affection." Simply meaning, no one deserves your love more than YOU do. There is the common belief that, in order to truly love others, you must first love yourself. Therefore, we can all agree humans deserve love. Now, can someone receive too much love? Is this even possible? I think most people would say no. The more love, the merrier!

Obviously humans deserve food, shelter, and water, which are the basic necessities of life. We know that. But what about money? Do they deserve money? Let me ask a question. If you have a job and thus you per-form work, do you expect to get paid? Of course you do.

Now, how did you pick, choose, or select the amount of money you get paid? My guess is when you were originally applying for the position, it had a certain base salary. You had a standard, perhaps a number in your mind, for how much money you 'needed' to make in order to pay your bills, eat food, and provide security for your family.

This was the case for me in my first 'big boy' job. I applied at Nationwide Insurance when I was 18 years old. This was in 2006. I applied for the position of call center representative. I knew my rent at the time was $650 a month. My car payment was $320 a month. My other various bills amounted to $600 a month which included food, cable, gas, insurance, and cell phone. This meant I needed at least $1,600 a month to make ends meet. After taxes, the job paid $1,800 a month. I thought 'perfect, I'll have an extra $200 for fun stuff' and this is why most people know the acronym JOB stands for Just Over Broke.

The point is, *many* people who search for a job do so based on how much money they need for bills. But how much money do you deserve? Most people will say something like, 'I don't deserve any money. I need to earn my living. I need to *prove* to my worth through hard work.'

But that's not entirely true, is it? I mean, you deserve some kind of money, otherwise you would just volunteer all of your time. You feel you *deserve something* because you put in 40-60 hours per week. The question then becomes 'How much money do you feel you deserve?'

And you want to know the epic answer? It's the amount of money you have **right now**. However much money you have right now is most likely how much money you subconsciously feel you deserve. I mean, it **has** to be, because that's how much you're making. And humans always want to get what they feel they deserve! It's called your standard of living.

If your mind says 'Well, I don't deserve *that much* money, because I'm not that smart, or I'm not good enough', then you are going to have a hell of a time getting more money.

How about we go through some examples. It will help this make more sense:

Let's say there are two people whose job is to fix hospital equipment.

Person One fixes 100 pieces of equipment in a year.

Person Two fixes 100 pieces of equipment in a year.

Person One loves the job and gets paid $40,000 a year in salary.

Person Two loves the job and gets paid $40,000 a year in salary.

However, Person Two starts thinking differently than Person One. Person Two reads some books and asks the question, 'How can I become more valuable?'

Person Two also comes up with a goal to make an extra $20,000 in cash before the end of the year for a down payment on a house.

Person Two has 1) invested in them-self by reading books and 2) set a defined goal with a specific number by a specific time.

Then Person Two gets to thinking. "I fixed 100 pieces of equipment last year, how could I become more efficient and better at my craft?" Person Two starts studying the specific job and getting better at their craft, and

Next year, Person One fixes 100 pieces of equipment

Next year, Person Two fixes 457 pieces of equipment

Person Two sees, feels, and believes in their massive improvement. Person Two also believes they deserve more money because they have increased their value tremendously. Here's the kicker Person Two then asks for more money showing the evidence of the improved work and efficiency.

Does Person Two actually deserve more money?

Of course. Remember, value = money.

Guess what happens in the above example? The company's CEO promotes Person Two so that person two can teach the other 500 employees how to become more efficient, which would cause the entire company to grow, thus adding more value, thus creating more money.

"Alright Jerremy, I'll bite. But what about the people who are scummy, mean, and greedy?"

Answer - They also feel like they deserve money. And they get it!

"Jerremy, if I just start *feeling* right now that I deserve more money, that doesn't mean I'm going to immediately get more."

You are correct. It's not immediate. It will not happen within hours. What will occur though is an imbalance. A see-saw effect. As you *truly begin to feel and believe that you actually deserve more money*, you will automatically seek paths that match that feeling.

"I'm not following you homie, I'm lost."

That's fair. Let me tell you a real story about a lady who I absolutely love. Her name is Roberta.

I hosted a meet and greet for some of my clients at a nice restaurant perched inside an upscale hotel in Chicago. We reserved a big table for about 12 people. The drinks flowed, the food was delectable, and it was a grand experience.

I sat to the left of Roberta for the whole dinner. I did my best to chat with each and every person while we were sitting down and mingling. There were various times throughout the dinner that Roberta was asking me questions, all of which revolved around how she could make more money. The questions were genuine and sincere, and sounded something like the following.

"I take care of my sick mother full-time and I need more money to help out with bills. What do you suggest?"

"I've been struggling trading the stock market and I have my account spread out over five XYZ stocks and their performance has been sub-par. What's your opinion on these five stocks?"

"What's your opinion on bonds? Should I put my mother's money in bonds to keep it safe and receive a return while I take care of her in her failing health?"

I did my best to answer each question in a non-licensed, non-financial advisor kind of way. But at the heart of each of my answers to her questions were more questions about her own self worth. Such as, what did *she* want out of the money? How much was enough? How much was too much? How much did she need? And better yet, how much did she deserve?

But I didn't ask that question until later in the night, after I'd had 2 or 3 'Old Fashioned's' and I was really jiving with everyone in attendance. At this point, I had hit full immersion and was at peak performance for the night. I began to inquire with Roberta.

"So Roberta, tell me what's your area of expertise again? I know you are in the medical field, right?"

"Yes. I work with autistic children. I'm an inpatient nurse and I help families who have disabled children. I help the families prepare food, exercise, and play with their children and provide mental stimulation and games."

"WOW! That is incredible! So you literally change and enrich lives every day?!"

"I guess you could say that. But it's beginning to wear me out. I see five or six patients a day, I drive about about two to three hours a day in between the homes of each patient, and it's really physically and emotionally draining work. I LOVE what I do, but after 12 years, and Jerremy as you know I'm no spring chicken, I just want to be better compensated for what I do."

At the time I was thinking something drastically different than what I was about to be told.

"How much do you make right now, doing this line of exceptional and rewarding work, Roberta?"

"I make $36,000 a year."

Friends, I was shocked! Like, jaw open, heart hurting in shock.

My reply was, "Why do you only make $36,000 a year? You live in Chicago! And you've been in this line of work for over a decade! I'm sure you had to get licensed and learn a very specific curriculum to perform your work."

"Oh, it's a struggle. I live in a small dingy apartment to save money, I drive a cheap car to cut down on bills, I never go out, I never drink, I eat small portions of food to cut costs, I love what I do, but I'm really looking to go to the next level."

"Okay, what's the next level for you, Roberta? How much would you like to make?"

"I would love to make just $50,000 a year. I think that's fair."

And here's where I dropped the haymaker. Remember, I'm honestly still flabbergasted that a woman of this caliber still makes so little. "Well, do you feel like you deserve $50,000 a year?"

Roberta exclaimed, "Oh heavens no! That's way too high for what I do. The children and families I help are low income and they can't afford much more than they pay me now."

"Do the families pay you directly, or does insurance help out?" *

Now, for congruency, I truly can't recall exactly what Roberta said about billing and the payment process for patients and families. I don't want speak for her in that regard and I want this book to be a surprise for her and others. Perhaps I'll ask in future editions. Either way, I recall it wasn't a horrendously burdensome approach for all families. Most just billed through insurance.

"Got ya. So you could technically charge more for your services? Because you offer a LOT!"

Roberta replied, "Yes, I could, but then I wouldn't get to impact so many children and help so many kids. Because the more I charge, the less people I would be able to help."

The next few paragraphs might be a tad controversial, but hang in there with me. Again, growing is uncomfortable. We will have to go through new mindset shifts and totally fresh paradigms to exponentially grow!

I truly feel in my heart of hearts the people in this world who deserve the most money usually do not receive adequate compensation. Most teachers are grossly under paid, as well as most nurses and others in the health care industry like Roberta. Then you have many in the public sector like firefighters and police and how about those who help protect the environment?

The truth is, in any industry you DO have certain ones who make LARGE sums of money, including the exact same list above. The top 1% of their field. You have race car drivers who do it for fun on Friday nights while they drive atop the red clay race tracks of South Georgia, and then you have Jeff Gordon. You have the lovely, kind, and generous teacher who pours liberation into the hearts of her students while teaching from a trailer with no air conditioning in New Mexico, and then you have Jordan Peterson, the professor of psychology at the University of Toronto.

What we have to understand is the world would unquestionably be a better place if everyone who actually deserved more money received it. However, we are the ones who receive what we feel we deserve. Just because YOU don't make as much money as you want, doesn't mean it is impossible to make more money in your field, sector, job or industry. I promise, someone, somewhere in the world who is in the same area of expertise is doing *very* well financially.

Here is how the conversation with Roberta continued:

Her previous comment was "Yes, I could, but then I wouldn't get to impact so many children and help so many kids. Because the more I charge, the less people

I would be able to help."

I replied, "Roberta, that is truly one of the most amazing, kind, and loving things I have ever heard. But we are at an impasse. Because here's the only way you will get more money. Either ask for more from your clients, or ask for more money from *someone else*. Companies, sponsorships, grants, donations, something."

Roberta said, "Oh, I could never ask for handouts."

I responded, "Well, you technically are asking for money when you work, right? You put in work and then you ask for money."

"Yes."

"So, just ask for more money. Double your rate tomorrow."

"But then I would lose SO many clients!"

"How much do you charge per hour, right now?"

"About $14 an hour."

"Okay, and how many clients do you see in a month?"

"In a month?! Wow, geeze, umm, about 25 a week, 100 a month."

"Do you charge for driving time, or only time while you are with your patient?"

"I only charge for the time I'm there, which is about 50 hours a week."

Again, my friends, I'm just shell shocked at this point. It's hard for me to put into words how saintlike this woman is. Roberta is one of those people you meet and you instantly smile because they are unique, funny, and filled with vibrance!

"So, Roberta, if you charged $28 an hour, how many clients do you think you would lose?"

"Probably about half, at least."

"Okay, so you have 100 clients per month now, and you make around $2,800 a month. If you doubled your rate and you had 50 clients per month, you would STILL make $2,800 a month, but you would work literally half as much."

She froze for about 20 seconds and then said

"Yeah, but no one would pay me that."

At this point I feel as if Mike Tyson punched me in the spleen. Roberta has NO CLUE how much she's worth! Because she's scared to ask! She is afraid that if she asks for more she will seem greedy and conceited because she's trying to take advantage of families who need her help.

This conversation lasted for a solid 30 minutes. I'll tell

you more about the exact ending of our chat later, but here are the big takeaways.

- Roberta had a scarcity mindset. She thought *just* because parents had a disabled child that they were automatically broke.

- Roberta loved what she did so much, and knew how important her role and work was, that she felt *bad* charging a lot for it because SO many people needed her help.

While it's an absolute certainty that there are many parents with autistic children who are financially strapped, emotionally stressed, and monetarily frustrated, there also *have* to be parents who are financially well off and want only the best for their child. They will pay top dollar to secure the best care available.

Does every parent in a situation like this *deserve* the best care possible? Absolutely!

But some can't afford the best care.

The above statement is true. But they can afford *some* care. And this is the big takeaway I had when speaking to Roberta. She had been doing this for 12 years! Meaning, she was an absolute professional! She was one of probably 10,000 nurses in the world who had 12 years of in-person experience working with autistic children. And she is probably what, one out of maybe ten in the Chicago area? I'm just throwing out numbers here, but that would make her quite valuable. At least, I could certainly see her value. But just because I can see someone's value that doesn't really mean anything. If that person doesn't believe it themself, then they certainly will not receive that value.

Let's ask the question this way.

Do you think there is at least one family, in or around Chicago, who would be willing to pay $10,000 a month for their child to receive exceptional loving care *each day*, every single month? I mean, the answer HAS to be yes. It's just math. It's basically a certainty. And that is just in Chicago! There are many more big cities here in the USA.

Circling back to our original number and goal of $14,000,000.

Ponder all of the amazing things that could be created if the best people you know and love in your life all had $14,687,594.04 in their bank account right now.

Consider all of the donations, charities, 501C-3, fundraisers, stock purchases, real estate investments, infrastructure plays, schools, websites, and scholarships that could be created to help future generations.

People rarely think they deserve what they have. YOU DO! You do deserve it, because you are worth it! If you feel you aren't worth it and you feel you don't deserve it, you simply will not get it. BAM!

I really like how Elizabeth Gilbert mentioned this topic in her book *Big Magic*. She said, "You must possess a fierce sense of personal entitlement, which I hope you learn to cultivate. I recognize the word *entitlement* has dreadfully negative connotations, but I'd like to appropriate it here and put it to good use, because you will never be able to create anything interesting out of your life if you don't believe that you're entitled to at least try."

She also mentioned in her book that the poet David Whyte "calls this sense of creative entitlement 'the arrogance of belonging' and he claims that it's an absolutely vital privilege to cultivate if you wish to interact more vividly with life."

Think about it. You are a good person right? If you are a good person, you *deserve* more money!! The world **needs** more incredible, loving, generous, thoughtful people who are burn-money-for-fun wealthy. Like walking your 10 pet lobsters with platinum chains on the sidewalk next to your home in Martha's Vineyard, *wealthy*. Actually buying the VIP tickets to the tent, air conditioning, and unlimited food and drink package at that festival you always wanted to attend, *wealthy*. Being able to have all of your bills on autopay because you aren't scared of getting a 'Non-Sufficient Funds', *wealthy*. Actually having a trust fund, wealthy. Knowing what a trust fund is, wealthy. Being on the cover of Fortune Magazine, *wealthy*.

Write down how much money you make per year:

_____

Write down how much money you feel you truly deserve per year:

_____

Write down why you feel you deserve that amount of money:

_____

_____

_____

_____

_____

_____

CHAPTER FIVE:
Money Is Currency

To reiterate how powerful words and definitions are in our brain, try this exercise out. Simply replace the word money with the word 'currency' in many of our common sayings and your internal reply will change. How you 'feel' will be different. For example, the love of currency is the root of all evil. What? Or, currency doesn't grow on trees. Or, I don't have enough currency to afford this item. It sounds weird, strange, and foreign.

Another example that could be used is "this pair of shoes costs 119 currency units." Sounds insane, I know, but the intriguing part of this exercise is it will remove how much something costs in your brain and therefore can help remove a subconscious hurdle.

Changing the word simply changes the whole impact of the statement, because we all grew up with certain stigmas, definitions, thoughts, and internal relationships with the word money. Of course, you'll also have an internal significance with even the 'slang' terms used in your part of the word for money. Here in the states you have "bucks" being a pretty common slang term for our money, which is US Dollars. In England they use "quid." You have "loon" and "toon" in Canada.

Whether I said, "this house costs $325,000 dollars" or "325,000 bucks," most of us here in the states would have no issue with this conversion of words. But if I said, "this house costs 325,000 currencies," now no one has any clue what I'm talking about - and neither does your BRAIN! If you want to trick your brain into quickly revolutionizing your feelings about money, just call it currencies in day to day situations. Remember, your brain is designed to protect you.

Mel Robbins gained massive notoriety for her "5 second rule" when she stated, "Hesitation is the kiss of death. You might hesitate for a just nanosecond, but that's all it takes. That one small hesitation triggers a mental system that's designed to stop you. And it happens in less than, you guessed it, five seconds."

Why does this matter? What is its importance? If I challenged you to save $200 dollars every week and put it into savings, the vast majority of humans would *immediately think* that's too much money. "I can't do that. I don't have that much." But if I challenged you to save 200 currency units every week and put it into savings, you'll have an easy 5 seconds to simply *think* that it's possible! For the first time in a long time, you can trick your brain from "That's too much, I don't have that," into "Maybe I could? I wonder how much that even is? What would I have to do in order to achieve that?"

Remember that money is just a word. It's a simple English word. But it's SO powerful. It has subliminal and subconscious definitions and meanings within each one of us, and if we want a better life, we have to change and shift those definitions and meanings. That is the goal of this entire book.

Recently it became one of my goals to explore some phrases and beliefs that other people have from their parts of the world. I made a recent friend of a super incredible guy who is a currency (FOREX) trader in Ireland. His name is Chris. When I was writing this book, I reached out to him on WhatsApp and I asked him, "Hey man, have you ever heard the term 'money doesn't grow on trees?' Is there a similar expression or phrase in Ireland that you heard when you were young?" His reply was astonishing. "Dude! I thought that was an Irish term! My mum used to tell me that on a daily basis."

About one year ago, I received a text message from a guy which said "Hey man! I am an Uber driver and one of my passengers last night told me to reach out to you and learn to trade the stock market." That was just the intro, but a few days later after a long exchange of texts we met at a Panera Bread restaurant. We spoke about the stock market for about 20 minutes until I asked him, "What kind of financial situation are you in? How much do you have to invest in the markets?" And this is where Nicholas went on to tell me he is from the Ivory Coast. He came to America about four years ago, and within weeks of him showing up and moving into an apartment, he had companies mailing him "free checks to cash." And he thought, 'This is great! This is why I moved to America! They literally mail you free money to use!' Well, as you know, he unfortunately fell into the trap of predatory lending. Companies were sending him personal loans, and he slipped into tons of debt.

I informed him at that point in our conversation that investing and trading the stock market was not the answer he was looking for, at least right now. Since he had very little to invest and a mountain of debt, our discussion went from trading the markets to the subjects of money, growth, and how to increase our value as a human so he could begin paying off his debts.

We chatted about ways to increase his value as an Uber driver, asking questions like, "How could you become one of the best Uber drivers ever, and what would that mean for you?" Later during our conversation I asked him, "Nick, have you ever heard the expression *money doesn't grow on trees?*"

He thought about it for a while and said, yes he had.

And then I asked, "Is it true? Does money grow on trees?"

And he said "It is true, yes."

I reminded him of those checks in the mail. I asked him, "How hard did you have to work for that money? It was just *given to you*, right? Now, of course it had a horrible interest rate, but what if you made a 400% return on that money? You would have been able to cover the super high interest rate."

At which point we discussed money, how it *truly does* grow on trees, and then I asked him, "Nick, tell me, what were some sayings in your country, similar to this one?"

He thought about it for a while and answered, "You can't just find money on the floor is kind of the translated version of what my parents would say a lot."

"Is that statement true?" I asked.

He thought it through and said, "Well, the other day I did find a quarter on the ground when getting gasoline," as he kind of laughed.

Exactly!

The big takeaway is of course that you can find money lying on the floor. Is it going to be enough money to provide a living? Well, that depends on how much you know about flooring. Could someone specialize in certain types of flooring? Could money be made in the buying and selling of wood floors, tile floors, concrete floors? Absolutely! Remember, it's all perception and what we perceive as true becomes real for us.

I saw a video on YouTube where a couple literally took pennies and glued thousands of them to the floor making a flooring entirely of the copper American currency. Since flooring is valued per square foot (at least here in the USA) they actually ended up *saving* money. That couple was originally considering some really nice hardwood, like a Brazilian Tigerwood or something, which was $3.79 per foot. And that only comes out to 379 pennies. Turns out, they actually saved currency by gluing the pennies to the floor. And it looked pretty cool, too.

Anyway, I want to give just another small anecdotal example showing you certainly can rest assured that we all *can find money* just lying on the floor, as long as we know its value and know where to look.

I was in an Uber ride with a sweet lady named Nora. She was from Lebanon. As we started chatting about careers and goals, I mentioned this book. She loved the idea and concept so much, it was just another boost and motivation to complete it! I also asked Nora, "What is a phrase you remember hearing while growing up about specifically money or currency?" Her answer was very similar to Nick's. She said, "My dad would often say you can't just go and find money on the streets. He was a very hard working man."

We spoke about it and discussed the phrase and its meaning. We chatted at length about how, similar to Nick's example, it depends! Yes, it's hard to just go out into the streets and look for and find enough money to live, but what about all of the shops on the streets, the vendors, the merchants, all of the people selling items and goods? All of the *street performers* who get a license (and some who don't) to perform on the streets to add value and entertainment to others, who in turn receive currency?

It all comes down to the fact that currency is every-where. We just have to look in order to find it. We have to know how to actually see the opportunities. Where many will see hurdles and obstacles, others will see profits and losses.

We have to train ourselves to think deeply and critically about any and all subjects. I like to call this "think-ing seven layers deep." There's rarely any benefit to believing the surface idea. There has to be something bigger, better, more meaningful if we give time to truly think about it.

If we do come to a place where we truly can no longer fashion an idea, or see an opportunity or find the silver lining, it's often best to ask someone who has already been there in the past. Mentors, guides, mental sherpas, they are everywhere. We simply have to look for the person and find a way to compensate them for their time (if they are alive). Most people forget that mentors can easily be authors, poets, kings, and queens that are no longer with us. As Robin Williams said in *Good Will Hunting*, "Those conversations can be pretty one sided." We can still learn and receive loads of wisdom bombs from a vast number of past leaders.

With the current internet at our fingertips, the sheer number of resources we have at our disposal is almost uncountable! That's such an exciting revelation to behold, if we want to learn it, it's there for our minds to uncover.

Write down your brain's first image that comes to mind when you hear or see the word money:

_____

Write down your brain's first image that comes to mind when you hear or see the word currency:

_____

Who are some good mentors that could help you learn more about money and finances?

_____

Do you have any friends, acquaintances, or contacts that are from a different part of the world?

_____

What are some quotes, phrases, or internal beliefs they might unknowingly have about money?

_____

_____

_____

_____

_____

If you can think of some, share them with me on my Twitter: @newsomenuggets

CHAPTER SIX:
Saying No, Like It Is Your Job

Wow! We have discussed so much already and we are only six chapters in?! How are you feeling? I trust you are wildly excited about all the new thoughts and ideas that are coming into your mind! This is where many people will start to become frightened, however. Why? Because this is all so new! Remember, most people never openly discuss money or how it impacts their lives or especially how they feel internally about money. Everyone simply knows they want more.

Here are some interesting thoughts I had when I first went down this mental rabbit hole. These are those fears and mental hurdles that always will come into your mind and life when you start contemplating all of the ways that exist to make more money. Some of the questions that flooded my mind were, "What if I make more money and become a drug addict? Or an alcoholic? What if I lose it all? What if I *change* and I become a *bad* person? What if I become greedy? What if I always get asked for money and give it all away because I'm too nice?"

Let's focus on that last one for a few paragraphs, because this subconscious belief is one very few people ever want to admit, yet it's the pink elephant in the room.

"What if I always get asked for money and give it all away because I'm too nice?"

Most people genuinely want to help others when they become rich and wealthy. Giving back, assisting, helping out the needy, the list goes on. BUT, they do realize that their amount of money is finite. We know money grows on trees, but as I will be describing shortly, you can cut a tree down and deprive yourself of all its bounty.

You probably get asked for money right now, don't you? Yet you are able to say no. Remind yourself, there have been times where you've walked along a downtown street and you've seen someone in obvious need of assistance. Their face had the deepest look of despair, but you just walked on by and your heart hurt.

You know it's not money they need. It's shelter or food or medical care, but money isn't the answer. Money isn't always the answer because money is a tool! If you try to use a hammer when tweezers are required, that pesky hair on your eyebrow most likely will not get plucked.

Here's a quote that really shook my world: "The difference between successful people and really successful people is that really successful people say no to almost everything." This is from Warren Buffett himself. What I struggled with until recently, I lived my life as a YES man. Saying yes to everyone and everything. It's still something I struggle with, but I have gotten better with it. That quote has revolutionized my way of thinking, because I see that while I want to be "really successful," I say yes to so many things. A book that helped me learn how to say no and schedule my time and priorities better was *Essentialism* by Greg McKeown.

When you become more successful, you will have more money trees! But for now, just forge ahead knowing you will have to say "no" more often. Just become used to it and start practicing it. It is okay to say "no". That doesn't make you a mean person. It doesn't make you evil or greedy, saying no is just an answer to a question.

Yet, this is one of the mental hurdles that will subconsciously hold a massive amount of people back from becoming wealthy, because they have a fear of turning into a greedy, evil person who has to say 'no' more frequently. Saying no is actually what wise people do.

Put yourself in the shoes of an apple farmer. What do you imagine the farmer's reply would be if someone asked him to cut down one of his apple trees in order to make it easier for them to pick apples? The farmer would never want someone to cut down their tree! It's the metaphor for someone asking you for money, and you knowing that money isn't going to help them. Their mindset is not ready for the money, because it will simply be thrown away and not appreciated. Even if it's a family member or friend, it's the wrong tool for the wrong time. You would actually be doing them a disservice. Your family member or friend might be addicted to spending money improperly. If they don't have a proper mindset or the mental fortitude to respect the tool of money, simply say no.

Realize that this could be a mother or father. A brother or sister. A cousin, niece, nephew or other relative. Is there anything wrong with them asking you? Nope! They see an opportunity! You should reward them for their line of thinking. This is important. You can even thank them for asking you. The conversation could go something like this:

Family member or friend: "Hey, so I heard you hit it big at [insert the way you will make more money] and I have this great idea for [insert an idea they have to strike it big] and I was hoping maybe you could help me out?"

You: "That is so thoughtful of you to ask. Thank you. I know that you were probably scared of asking and it takes courage, however, I am not an expert in [insert their idea to strike it big] and per my financial plan, I am only allowed to take financial risks in an area where I'm an expert."

Now, what if *you are* an expert in what they are asking money for? Perhaps you flip houses and have absolutely crushed it in recent years. Well, then you will know if they are presenting you with a good deal. You will have the ability to actually judge, "Is this a good idea?'

Most often, when you are approached from anyone asking you for money, it will be for something of which you are not a specialist. Perhaps it is a fund raiser, raising money for endangered gorillas. If you find yourself comfortable saying and using the term, "It's not in my financial plan to take risks in an area where I'm an expert," it means you've thought it through.

If you LOVE gorillas and it's been your mission to help them, fantastic! Then you are now presented with an opportunity to learn more about how you can help. Get as many details as you can about the donation or offer, and take a calculated approach.

The truth is, when you have more money, you simply will receive countless opportunities to spend it. Money LOVES to work. It loves to be spent, circulated and used. This means you will receive loads of opportunities to put it to work. But keep in mind what Bret Stephens said, "Generosity is a virtue, but unlimited generosity is a fast route to bankruptcy."

This practice of saying no simply gives you the opportunity, the freedom, and the path to focus on what matters most to YOU. It's perfectly fine and acceptable to help those in need, to give, and to be generous. I encourage you, constantly look for new ways to show generosity and to truly feel it.

Generosity is a feeling that when it occupies the soul, there is no room for any other feelings. It's all-encompassing. There's true warmth in generosity. Therefore, we have to protect our tree. Just like it's possible to pick all the apples from a tree, it's possible to spend more money than you make or have. Sure, you can always go create more money by adding more value, but trees are *living* things. They are alive! They can be mistreated, and so can your trees of money. If you never water them, they can die. If the trees are planted in the wrong soil, they can wither and produce low quality fruit. No sunlight, I heard, is a problem for trees as well. Just like the physical tree, the money tree in your mind has to be kept alive. Remember, money is everywhere. It's our thoughts and beliefs that determine how much we have and what we do with it.

Remember that time you were at work, and *'that one person'* came up to you and started talking to you? You already aren't super fond of this person. Their style is kind of shabby, their breath isn't wonderful, their teeth are kind of jaggy, their whole energy has this 'Oscar the Grouch' flair and you have work to do. And the whole time, you knew they were going to ask you a question and you were saying no internally, but when they finished, you said yes to their request? You know why this occurs right? Because you don't want to hurt their feelings. As humans we've associated yes as good and no as bad.

We have to teach that voice to say **no** both internally, which it has no issue doing, and **no** out loud when we must. Our understanding has to become that no is simply an answer to a question. If someone asks you to buy a product that you don't want, nor would this product bring value to your life, simply say "no."

How weird is that? Even when you read that, your brain thought 'Wow, just saying no would be rude. I would have to say no thank you.' HAHA. Why is that? They are asking you for money or time, which are both the only tools we can ever use to grow. That's it. Done. Finished, end of discussion. We can either use time or money. That person is requesting a beautiful tool from you and it's your tool!

I like how Stephanie Lahart put it: "Let today mark a new beginning for you. Give yourself permission to say NO without feeling guilty, mean, or selfish. Anybody who gets upset and/or expects you to say YES all of the time clearly doesn't have your best interest at heart. Always remember: You have a right to say NO without having to explain yourself. Be at peace with your decisions."

And my boy Amit Kalantri said, "Real freedom is saying 'no' without giving a reason."

How powerful is that?! That might become my new favorite quote next month. How many times has a friend asked you to a dinner party and it wasn't in your budget, but you said yes anyway just to put it on a credit card? Or your younger cousin asked you to pay for his tuxedo to his own wedding because he didn't have the money, even though he has a job? Or the time you bought that one course on the phone because the salesperson was pushy and really good at their job and you more or less agreed to the purchase simply to get rid of the person? There goes $399, right down the tubes.

Remember, your brain internally is terrified of displeasing people. And your brain *knows for a 100% certainty*, when you become more rich and wealthy, folks will be asking you for money. And if your answer is always yes, rather than no, you will run out of money. And that would be failure. And your brain doesn't want failure, so it's much easier just not having the money!

BOOM! REVELATION people! THROW your hands in the air!

Anytime I'm at a live event, this is the time people go crazy. Think about that even for just a few minutes. Your brain, energy and mind are self sabotaging your success because they don't want to go through the discomfort of saying no to friends, family, or aggressive sales people you are not fond of anyway. The surprising fact is, your brain is already very good at saying no. As mentioned earlier, your brain says no all the time. It is usually internally, rarely out loud and often it says no to your wonderful ideas because of some hidden, underlying fear. And that fear is displeasing someone, most likely.

Once you tell your brain that *it's going to happen* it will slowly begin accepting the certainty, and you have a better shot of money coming into your life. You will turn people off. You will say no to actual humans, with your mouth or hands. There will definitely be times and instances where you don't give someone money and that might upset or offend them. Guess what, people get offended.

I've seen people get offended because they didn't receive *enough* money. They held out for another contract, or didn't sign the paper, or didn't cash the check. Is that a bad thing? Nope. They know what they wanted and *they* had the power to say no. The truth is, people often just take offense.

Kris Carr once said, "You can't please everyone. When you're too focused on living up to other people's standards, you aren't spending enough time raising your own. Some people may whisper, complain and judge. But for the most part, it's all in your head. People care less about your actions than you think. Why? They have their own problems!"

Which means, you'll probably even upset family members. Heaven forbid, maybe even your immediate family! GASP. Am I saying, even your parents might ask for money? Especially your parents! Your brain is really terrified of this one.

"Jerremy, are you saying that I shouldn't give money to my parents?"

I'm certainly not saying you shouldn't. Ha ha

What I'm saying is, do not give them all of it. I'm

definitely saying there's a chance they will ask for it OR better yet, throw out weird vibes and energies which might make you feel bad about having money. It's not their fault. Remember, they too grew up believing an exorbitant amount of untruths about money. As great as your parents are, it's likely that they also have a vast amount of limiting beliefs about money. Why? Because they got it from *their* parents.

The best thing to do when this happens is to make an attempt to help your parents out of the rut. Send them books, like this one, tapes, YouTube videos, CDs, DVDs, buy them tickets to seminars, just get their brain involved in the repair process!

It's such a liberating feeling when you can openly discuss money and finances with your parents! Just being able to chat with family and especially parents about budgets, future visions, cash flow, income streams, *good debt* and *bad debt*, sets up the large possibility of creating future legacies and generational wealth for your family.

Since we are on the topic, there is a healthy chance you have children. What are the two huge issues most families and parents just totally skirt? Sex and money, of course. Uhh, why do *the two best things ever* constantly get overlooked and under discussed? It's a shame. Take the route of communicating! Discuss money with your children. Even at a young age, they need to know how it works.

I've heard from numerous parents their fear of discussing money is because they are never that financially sound. So, why should their kids listen to them? What if their kids ask them other questions they don't know the answer to? WONDERFUL! That is called learning people! HA HA. We can no longer be afraid of not knowing something. If you are unaware of an answer, tell your kid, "Hey, I really am not sure. What a great question. Let's go find out together." Your child will emulate you in many ways. And if you are bad at finances, the chances are, your kid will be as well. But if you as a parent do not start speaking with your kid early and often about the things that matter in life, someone else will.

Beth Koblinger is a wonderful author and exceptional advocate for finances and helping your children learn early. She said "It's okay if you are not a millionaire - you can still easily teach your kids about budgeting and basic money concepts. And if you still feel inadequate as a teacher, good! Go learn with them. Togetherness in learning, I'm all for that!"

Do you recall your parents ever sitting down and discussing money with you in detail?

_____

If yes, what did you all talk about?

_____

If no, why do you think they avoided that discussion?

_____

Who in your family would be the first to ask you for money, if you received $1,000,000 extra in the next year from your hard work and value adding?

_____

_____

Would you feel weird inside saying 'no' versus 'no thank you' and if yes, why?

_____

_____

Do you feel your family members would love you less if you did not give them money?

_____

_____

CHAPTER SEVEN:
Ways To Protect Your
Newly Found Money Tree

It might be surprising, but I didn't realize until I was in my early 20's that even wealthy people have a budget. I always thought internally, "They have so much money, they can buy whatever they want." As mentioned previously, tons of folks have a negative perception on rich people. They think rich people are stingy, stuck up, and non-giving. It's probably because of a movie, film, YouTube video, meme, or literal instance where a rich person walks past someone in need and doesn't help them or give them money.

But you have done that too, right? You have driven by that person who was holding that sign looking sad, frightened, scared, and upset, and you did absolutely nothing. You've walked by that person who was lying on the ground when it was cold outside and they were sleeping on and under cardboard to stay warm. I know you have. It happens to all of us.

I certainly have been in those situations where I am just unable to help at that moment. I feel horrible each time, but I know it actually is physically impossible to help every single person in this world. I certainly scope out the situation, surroundings and circumstances to see what I can do to help and assist. Do they need directions to a homeless shelter? Do they need food, water, wet wipes, a place to stay, a hug, handshake, what do they need or want? I can say that money is rarely the answer.

Money is a tool. And if used improperly, it simply will not work or create solutions to problems. Think of money like a fire. A fire can keep you warm, it can cook food, ward off baboons in certain Disney films, it can be exciting like in a firework, or it can be devastating like a forest fire that ravages homes and properties and takes lives. Fire is absolutely a tool. So is money. Both can be used incorrectly. If someone is a drug addict, money rarely solves the issue. If someone is homeless, money rarely solves the issue.

Back to budgets, because that was a bit of a tangent. Rich people are usually quite smart. That's how they became well-off. And rich people know the above situations are often accurate. You probably have seen someone you thought was rich not give to a singular person in need, but you probably didn't see the same person make a $10,000 donation to the organization that helps those in need. Wealthy people budget. It's as simple as that. And budgeting is easy spend less than you make.

You can get more strict with it, and I suggest you do, especially early on in the journey. You need to know how much money you spend on every activity. Most banks will do this for you. Any good bank has a budgeting section where you can set alerts, alarms, or text messages if you are spending too much in a given category.

When I was younger I *loved* booze. Probably too much and I realized it early. One of the first things I did with my budget was only allocate $100 for alcohol for a whole month! For some, that is shockingly high and for others ha ha, and you know who you are, that will be wildly low. I also determined how much I need to spend on food per month, entertainment, clothing, I mean, I created a legit budget.

This really is something you want to do. One thing I help clients with all the time is to carve out extra money and time that they didn't know they were spending frivolously. A fun fear your brain has created is that of running out of money. I say 'fun' because it's both a conscious and subconscious fear.

Here is an example: Your brain doesn't want to lose. No one actually likes losing, ever. And if you have not shown your brain that you can manage money wisely and effectively, it knows, often rightfully so, that if you receive all the money you could ever want, it will eventually be gone. Poof, squandered. Because a tree can only produce so much fruit. You can always get more trees, but there will be a time where you sow and where you harvest. Bottom line, it's certainly possible to spend more than you make.

There can come a point where the scale gets skewed. If your net worth is $100,000,000,000, it's going to be very hard to spend all of that. But it's possible! For most humans out there I'm truly hoping we will be floating around that $100,000,000 mark, which can *easily* be spent. LOL! - that's right. I had to drop one of those in the book.

Creating a budget is a great way to begin to show your brain that you can handle money. It needs to be confident that you will not just blow it. As Chris Rock said on stage once, "Wealth gets passed on from generation to generation rich is something you can lose during a crazy summer and a drug addiction."

It's wildly true. Wealth is money which creates more

money constantly and consistently. It's because there are processes and procedures in place that keep the money churning. It's similar to constantly planting, watering, taking care of, and harvesting more and more trees. We have to think about where our money is going and what's happening with it. Are we spending it, or investing it? When we buy something, are we a consumer or an owner? Do we own or do we buy?

There are countless schools of thought on this topic! Some mentors I follow say 'do not buy a home until you are 40 with a family. Keep building cash until you know exactly what to do with it.' Other mentors say, "Own real estate and pay it off quicker with a first position Home Equity Line of Credit (HELOC)". Others say, "Save your 20%, buy a house, rehab it, live in it for 2 years, fix it up, sell it, and use the cash to do it again and continue fixing and flipping houses for 4-8 years. Save up and start flipping homes.'

Who do you listen do? Which path do you take?

The answer: which one makes sense to you right now?

At some point, we have to chose, we have to make a decision, and we have to go with it. No one knows if the decision is the right or wrong one until later. If the decision turned out to be the wrong one or simply not the best choice, learn from it, regroup, and move forward.

When picking a path, a direction, you will begin a certain chapter in your life. **Eric Thomas says "If you want a hard life, do what's easy. If you want an easy life, do what's hard."**

What the heck does that mean? Tons. I could do a whole book on just that quote. Hmmm. Not a bad idea. BUT, I'll certainly do a quote of the week video about it.

Here's my take on that quote. It seems obvious as we can easily say there are certain mentors, information, books, approaches and suggestions that will be less work than others. Obviously saving 20% down for a home is *harder* than buying one through Federal Housing Administration (FHA), which is just a 3.5% down payment. And of course renting is actually massively easier than buying a home, especially if you are self-employed. Both have various pros and cons. My advice, just research it all. Watch YouTube videos, Tweet at me @newsomenuggets, and we can chat about which might be best for you. I'll help guide you towards the best choices.

The most important lesson is to know how much you spend, and on what areas of your life. Some have said, "What you spend most of your money on can show you what you find most important in you life."

Now, obviously the majority of people will be spending

most of their money on their home. I get that. Makes tons of sense. But look closely at what else you spend money on. How much do you spend on alcohol per month, relative to buying books? Just that one small metric alone might shock you.

Since marijuana is now legal in the vast amount of places that people might be reading this book, how much do you spend on marijuana, per month? Or sweets? Or cigarettes? Or cigars? Or other drugs? Simply, how much money do you spend on vices and 'escapes?' If the answer is none, I can assure you that you are better disciplined financially than the vast majority of humans on this planet.

Another cost that really inhibits people from financial freedom is their transportation. Too many people factor in just the cost of their vehicle. You also have to consider gas, maintenance, insurance, tag renewal, and the small cost of keeping it clean and tidy.

Unfortunately, this becomes a trap for far too many people. Someone will purchase a super cheap vehicle that constantly breaks down, which in turn costs money to repair, and they will not keep their insurance or tags up to date because it costs too much money, which in the long run will cost them massively if they get pulled over. Speeding tickets, DUIs, parking tickets, and other random bills will really stack up! Avoid this trap by taking care of your vehicle, keeping everything clean, tidy, and up-to-date. And of course, never drive intoxicated, don't drive recklessly, and don't speed! Getting just one ticket can increase your insurance cost significantly, and is often an extra $150-$350 that you totally didn't anticipate spending. This lifestyle can keep many people poor. Speaking of, I'm going to go get my registration renewed right now! I'm heading out the door to get that taken care of.

Go through your spending and see what 'sectors' of your life you can reasonably cut back in and increase spending in other areas, such as investing in yourself and your future. This practice is to prove to your brain that you are able to handle larger sums of money. The more you can reassure yourself and your internal mind that you are able to handle money, protect it, and spend it appropriately, the more likely you are to receive more of it!

Do you have a budget?

_____

What is one area in your life you admittedly spend too much money?

_____

What is one area in your life where you spend too little money?

_____

What happens to be something you've never spent money on, but you should?

_____

CHAPTER EIGHT:
The Actual Written Formula For Insane Success

We are taught by society to relate jobs with money. If I get a better job, I get more money. So is it impossible then to get an inheritance from a loved one who has passed? Is it unattainable to be the person who *creates* a business, and therefore jobs, for others? Is it fictitious to write that book, with that idea, concept and story that has never been told before, which circulates earth wide and produces hundreds of millions of dollars in revenue? Is it ludicrous to think anyone could make money by simply being really funny and crafting jokes and tales in such a way that vast audiences crave more?

We must know that anyone can craft money from any circumstance. Michael Phelps literally is worth around $55 million dollars because he *swims faster than everyone else in the world.* Can you imagine? I hope you *can* imagine, because it's true and it happened. Usain Bolt is simply faster than every single human on this planet, and he gets paid staggering sums to be fast.

Now, I want to be clear; I totally realize there is more to their wealth than one simple skill. It is the honing of that skill, the craftsmanship of that ability, the focusing on that muse that created such world-class athletes. But it's TRUE and it is possible!

Tom Brady throws a leather ball really well and gets paid exorbitant fees for doing so. Is that *literally* all he does? Of course not. Usain doesn't only run fast, and Michael doesn't only swim. These people are rewarded in public for what they've relentlessly practiced in private. All of this came from their thoughts. At one point in their lives, before it actually occurred, I am 100% confident all three men noted above visualized their success. They wanted it to occur and they willed it to happen through focused effort and determination.

Ninety-four year old Harriette Thompson became the oldest woman to complete a half marathon with her 3:42:56 finish at the Rock N' Roll San Diego Half Marathon back on June 4th, 2017. In the next few years, I expect that record to be broken, because she broke the previous record which was held by Gladys Burrill, who ran a half marathon at 93 years old in 2012.

What does any of this have to do with money?

Simple. Anyone can get more money at any time. It's very possible. You have to believe that with your whole soul. Because *anyone* can accomplish *anything* with the right formula. I love what Kyle Maynard said once in one of his many inspirational videos. He's the gentleman who climbed Mount Kilimanjaro, *and* also happens to have no legs or arms. In a video he said, "Anything is possible' is a lie. I love the spirit of that. I don't believe it's true. Anything is possible, cool, go bench press 10,000 pounds. What's more effective is to truly know our limits. And to truly know our limits, we have to go test them."

What's beautiful about that is within, it contains many truths. I mean, is 'anything' really possible? Humans can't fly, right? As much as we would like to, it is physically impossible. To which someone might say, but let me build a plane! It's a perfect representation of the mindset. There are certain human impossibilities that lay within our physical frames. We can't fly, we can't breathe underwater, we can't jump 400 feet in the air, we can't bench press 10,000 pounds, we can't jump off of a 100-story building and survive the fall.

Yet, humans have done all of the above. We have simply constructed devices, machines and apparatuses to help us with such feats. The issue is many of the impossibilities we believe day to day are internal and mentally constructed, but backed by no laws of physics.

Here is the simple formula that will help produce 99.9% of your wants, dreams, goals and aspirations.

1. You take time to think about something extremely specific

2. You physically write down why you want to achieve that extremely specific task.

3. You then determine whether it has been done before (hint, most things have). If it has, go research the who, what, when, where, and of course, how.

4. You begin actually writing down the steps and actions you will take on the course to achieving what you outlined in #1.

5. You do whatever is required each day and week until the goal is accomplished. Start telling people about your goals and dreams. Put it out into energies of this world and watch it begin to unfold.

Let's look at an example.

Pretend you are yourself, back many moons ago, when you are 15 years old and you want to win the state wrestling competition at your school.

Well, Step #1 is already finished. You have something extremely specific that you want to accomplish.

Now, Step #2, physically write it down somewhere. This could be in a notebook or on a simple piece of paper that you carry with you daily, or you could laminate it and place it on your fridge. Write it on your mirror or whatever it takes to remind you of the task at hand.

The unfortunate news? Many people fail to even make it this far into the formula.

Step #3: 'Has it been done before?' Yep, we can certainly say that a state wrestling competition has been won before, which is wonderful! Because now we can find someone who has achieved this in the past and ask incredible questions. Questions like, "What was the main reason you wanted this accomplishment?" "What was your training regimen like?" "Did you have a specific diet?" "Did you have any rituals that helped you get in the zone?" "How many times did you fail?" "Who was your role model?"

This is just a general list of questions, of course, but a great place to start.

Step #4: Is another repeat of Step #2. Physically taking your hand along with a pen or pencil and placing it against paper and writing down your steps. This act creates waves and energies that have shaped history and will continue to do so! The expression 'the pen is mightier than the sword' carries much weight.

Step #4 is where you determine your 'WHY' and 'I WILL' and 'I AM' statements. Why do you want this goal? What will you do in order to achieve it? Who will you become in the process? Who are you now? Create an identity! I'm a Spectacular Spartan, a warrior of the highest regard, an unstoppable force on the wrestling mat! You have to invoke power, beliefs, conviction, something that gets you fired up! A phrase and belief that scares you a little bit.

Just now, when you read the word 'unstoppable,' your brain might have gone 'well, yeah, but I'm not truly unstoppable. There's a good chance I'll lose at some point.' There's that doubt creeping in! Who says you have to lose? Is it impossible to go undefeated? If the answer is no, believe that it will happen to you. And if you do lose, as mentioned before, that's okay. Losing is not failing. Unstoppable doesn't need to mean undefeated. Any word *can mean* whatever you want them to. And keep in mind, they will.

Words carry so much weight! Everything we know, think, and believe starts with the words of our language that we are taught. Words construct phrases, and phrases often shape our life!

As you might have guessed, even less people will make it this far. Between Step #4 and Step #5 is where only those who desire it most will win. Only the people with the strongest why in their hearts, with the clearest vision and purpose, will even make it this far. Four simple, easy steps. Two of which can be accomplished in under five minutes. Five minutes of time, my friend, will hold the majority of people back even once they know the secret formula.

Step #5 is where 90% of people will fail, because it's truly hard. Doing anything good is usually hard. Jim Rohn once said, "Doing what we must to succeed is easy, but not doing it is even easier." The statistics of the amount of people who start and fail at most things is staggering. It's not because of the resources, it's because of the resourcefulness. The grind, the grit, the determination, the discipline, it all boils down to 'How bad do you want it?' However, the previous example is a physical goal. Let's run through one that is solely a money goal.

In this example you are a stay at home parent. Your spouse works full-time, and you have the wildly busy schedule of taking care of the home. You know, every-thing in it. The food, the clothes, children are probably demolishing those two things, then we have the cleaning, the driving, the schedules. You get the picture. And in this example, let us create a goal where this person generates 100,000 extra currencies a year! Of course, this sounds like an absolute dream for most. Something totally outlandish. No way could I ever make that much money. Well, we know it's not impossible because people have done it before.

Therefore we have our specific goal, the Step #1 in this formula. Make 100,000 of extra currencies this year. And then, Step #2, you write it down somewhere. This is the part where you literally with your hand, mouth, feet, or by any other means, write down this goal. Then Step #3, you start doing some research. Remember, it all comes down to value. Keep in mind what my boy Abraham Lincoln said, "Do not believe everything you see on the internet."

If you do find yourself in this exact situation, the one where you are a stay at home parent who would love nothing more than creating 100,000 extra currency units a year, please know that people will prey on you. The internet is filled with scams, fake stories and altered testimonials to get desperate people to spend money on trash courses and products.

The value comes in because your goal is to find actual people who did it, not products. Find role models online or in books, magazines, or blogs. People that are real and genuine. You will know who they are! And if you need help, use the internet. Use review boards and start asking around and remember, it's okay to say no. If you come across a webinar, website, or product that's trying to sell you the dream, but all you have to do is buy $1,000 worth of product and then sell that $1,000 of product and make $10,000, beware. I totally understand that you have to pay to receive things. Just make sure it's something you really want to receive. Ensure it's a path you feel good about. And be strong enough to say no if it's not. You might get numerous phone calls or emails *begging* you to buy a product or a course. I'm certainly not saying you shouldn't buy a course. In fact, there are thousands of extremely reputable, helpful and motivating courses online. Just be smart and do your research. Take time to make a decision.

From there we have various books, programs, seminars, and classes which will be ridiculously helpful. One thing that has helped me when finding a course and instructor is buying their book (if they have one) or downloading their free e-book, which they most likely have, and reading it. I do this because I want to see if I like *their voice*. You know, their narration and overall discussion. If you like them after spending an hour or two going through their information, then consider budgeting for their product.

One of my sayings is, "Everything works, just not all the time." Meaning, it doesn't matter if you are learning to sell chocolate, oils, real estate, cars, candy bars, software, or perhaps you're learning to code, day trade, conduct real estate transactions, teaching English to Chinese children, flipping products on Ebay, or doing drop shipping - *everything* has its pros and cons. All of it will take work.

And that's why we have Steps #4 and #5.

You have to know what you are going to do, which steps you are going to take, when you are going to take them, and where your exact steps will land.

You have to build out your dream. Really give it thought. Sit down with a bottle (or glass) of wine or hit a good five mile hike, enjoy an invigorating massage, play a sport, visit a homeless shelter, *do something* to get the vibes going! Ponder, deliberate, actually *think with your brain* and determine if there's any future in what you want to work on.

Do you like any of the aforementioned paths? Does flipping furniture on Ebay sound appealing to you? Maybe you want to buy and sell nice watches? Or nice cars, old books, day trade, sell houses the paths are endless.

Examine this for a moment. What is your mind saying right now? It's probably the subconscious part. You might be able to barely hear it in your mind, very softly and quietly. It likely will not be a loud voice, but at some point while reading through the ideas you might have heard it, 'No, this isn't going to work. I can't do this. I don't have the money to spend. I'm not smart enough. I'm not good enough. I don't know anything about real estate. I don't know anything about the stock market. I don't know anything about selling." Tons of self doubt, pity, and negativity will creep into your mind initially. What is truly wild is that your brain is totally comfortable saying no internally. You can say no quietly all the time, maybe even under your breath.

As you begin the journey of asking for money and feeling you deserve more monetary rewards for your hard work, you will find that the universe will throw other paths your way. It will find out how badly you actually want what you said you wanted.

Continuing with our example of the stay at home parent who wants to make 100,000 of additional currencies in a year's time, but something comes up, perhaps a part-time job, where they can make 10,000 extra currencies per year, will they take it? Keep in mind, this 10,000 currencies per year job has very little upside or room for growth. Selling knives or Christian coloring books comes to mind. Is there anything wrong with that? Nope. Not in the slightest. One can learn loads of skills from something like this. But is it what you want? Are you excited by it? Does it drive you? And did you ask for it?

"Jerremy, are you telling me, that if I want to make 100,000 extra currencies per year, I shouldn't settle for something that's going to pay me 50,000 extra per year?"

I am telling you that the universe will give you what you ask of it.

"Then you are saying, all I have to do is ask for an extra 100,000 extra currencies per year, and poof, tomorrow my bank account will have that much more money?"

I am telling you that if you can find a way to help 100,000 people, the odds of you having 100,000 extra in your bank account will increase dramatically.

See, right there! That voice in your head that said in your brain, "100,000 people? How the heck am I going to do that? I only have 253 friends on Facebook." That's the voice we have to retrain. There are 100,000 people that you can connect with. It's just going to be really difficult. I mean, can you think of a nearby city that has 100,000 residents? Is it possible for you to go literally door to door 100,000 times? The answer is yes. In my lifetime I probably have knocked on 100,000 doors. I have had 91,187 slammed in my face at one point or another, but I tried! I got out there. I did it. I learned.

In the same above example, let's pretend the stay at home spouse was exceptional with children and loved teaching, helping, caring, and providing for them. Could that person go door to door and offer their services as a tutor, nanny, au pair, coach, helper or simply an assistant? Absolutely. Is it possible for that stay at home spouse to make an additional 100,000 a year with those services? Sure. Will it be easy? Nope. Would you have to cater towards a certain clientele? Yep.

But it's possible! That's the point I'm trying to make. It can be done. Our brains are trained to say no internally, but say yes externally. Far too often we will only see the hurdles, with no way over them. They are able to be overcome! Just know it takes a different line of thinking and an alternate approach, but it will be doable!

Physically write down one BIG goal you 100% will accomplish in the next eight months:

_____

_____

Do you know of anyone who has ever achieved said goal? (Hint: It's probably been accomplished.)

_____

_____

Does that person or group have books, videos, seminars, webinars or any material online which you can research on how to achieve the goal you want?

_____

_____

Why do you want to achieve this goal?

_____

_____

CHAPTER NINE:
What Is Our Relationship
With Money

I hope you are ready for the culmination! I like to finish strong! Potentially saving the best for last, I have a mysterious, auspicious, intangible, and crucial discussion in the next series of words and pages.

It's time to dive into our relationship with money. How we feel about its energy, its uses, and its purpose. And the best way is to reveal we still have tons of sayings, phrases, quotes, thoughts, and maybe even slogans that could hold us back from what we seek. You are reading this book because you want more money! The easiest way to begin accomplishing that goal is by changing the way we think about money, its flow, its energies.

Because money is created and if anything is created, it has energy. And if we know the energy, we can attract it.

Money is not that important.

How about we just stop saying this altogether. There is no need to kid yourself. This is not a joke. Money is important. Money *knows* it's important and it wants to be treated with respect and reverence.

Are you in a relationship with someone right now? The answer is most likely a yes. Even if you are totally single, you probably still have children, pets, friends, and loved ones. You are in a relationship with someone, somewhere. Perhaps it is a platonic and not a romantic relationship, but I digress.

How would that individual feel if every so often you said out loud, "You aren't that important to me?" I would imagine you likely would hurt their feelings pretty often. Eventually they would no longer want to be around you. Money is the same. It has an energy associated with it. If you think money is not important, you are sending out the vibes that you don't like it and you don't want to spend time with it.

Money is so important! Have you tried living without the use of money at all? Can you imagine how tough that would be? And yet I hear this all the time. Someone will say to me, "Look, I know money isn't that important, and I'm not trying to be greedy or anything, I would just love help growing my business." One of my first replies is often, "Let's work on your relationship with money first. You aren't greedy, and money is important! That's why you want to grow your business, because you want more money."

"No, I only want to help other people! I don't care about money."

I say, "Then do it for free."

"Well, then I wouldn't be able to provide for my family. I need an income."

"Sounds like you want to help tons of people AND make loads of money. Is that a bad thing?"

"Look, I'm not trying to be greedy but yes, I would love more money."

Can you see and almost *feel* that person's energy? They are almost shoving money away, giving it the cold shoulder. Embrace it. Understand if you do an incredible job at *pretty much anything*, you deserve to be rewarded for it.

That brings me back to my girl, Roberta.

If you want more money, you have to accept your skills. You have to realize you can't be a mother (or father) to all children. Mother Teresa didn't help every single human on this earth, neither did Martin Luther King Jr., Mahatma Gandhi, Muhammad, Moses or Jesus Christ. Their calling wasn't money related but they did use money as a tool. Each figure knew how to appropriately ask for money, or create money or discuss money to simply use it for good.

If you are building something, a legacy perhaps, you will need certain tools. And one of those tools will be money. Roberta, if you are reading this, know that I love you dearly and I SEE your value! Go out and ask for it and know that you have put in the time, effort, skills and learning to receive fair compensation for what you do.

"Don't put all of your eggs in one basket."

I love this one! There is some controversy over the origin of the phrase; however, this expression is most commonly attributed to Miguel Cervantes, who wrote Don Quixote in 1605.

Ponder how this one saying, that vast droves of people use - could impact your spending, saving, and growing. An example could be you say out loud to a friend "I really want to buy that house, but it will eat up my savings." Someone else's answer to you, "Don't put all your eggs in one basket. It's probably better to wait until you've saved a bit more." This quote is one straight from the ideals of scarcity. Although I fully understand its meaning and benefit, how about we dissect it some.

First, is it really *all* of your eggs? What if you had 10,000 currency units just sitting in a savings account, and an opportunity comes along that costs 10,000 of those currency units. Is this putting all of your eggs in one basket? We first must ask, what are the chances that you can lose the entire 10,000 currencies? Are you buying an asset or a liability?

Here are two more examples:

Consider you are a watch expert. You love watches. You study them, you know how to repair them, you know how they work, you know their history. Watches are a deep and intimate passion of yours. You find a watch for sale by owner online and this watch is in pristine condition. The person is selling it because it was a gift given by a former significant other, so they no longer want it. Sale price is 9,995 currencies, and you are wildly confident it can be sold for 14,000 currency units on another website. In fact, you pull up various examples of the same or similar watch on sale between 12,000 - 15,000 currency units. You plan your worst case scenario: buy it for 9,995 currencies, but can't sell it for a few weeks or months, hire a photographer to take great pictures of it, get it polished by the local jeweler - spend 200 to 400 currencies for that and then sell it *eventually* for 10,000 currencies So, you scratch essentially. Break even. BUT, you got some great pictures of you wearing a really nice watch out of the deal. Potentially, you even got to wear this watch playing poker with friends, or at a cigar lounge, or during a business deal. Someone noticed it and liked it, and asked you about it and made inquiries. You could have drummed up some business from wearing this watch!

That might have been a game changer. Maybe you felt more pride or a sense of accomplishment because of this singular watch and that helped you in your presentation. Whatever occurred, your worst case scenario wasn't actually that bad.

On the flip side, let's present a similar case study. Let's remove all that hard work and research that went into the purchase. You are walking through The Bellagio Resort in Las Vegas, and you spot a watch that just takes your breath away. So you buy it at retail - ouch. And then you proceed to show it off to everyone who is with you, bragging about how cool the watch is. You make sure everyone knows how much you spent on it, and then you drink to excess that night, blacking out, and you totally lose the watch without a shred of recollection as to where you lost said watch.

CLASSIC.

In both situations the same amount of coinage was spent. But one approach viewed the transition as an asset, and the other, a liability. It could have even been the same watch! The wild fact is, stories like this happen all the time. Similar route, but two different outcomes because of the focus.

I could reproduce the exact same examples above with cars, clothes, shoes, guns, furniture, stocks, bond. Just money in general. The more you know about something, the better chance you will make the right decisions with it. Which leads us back to 'all of your eggs.'

The amount of times it will literally be every single 'egg' you own should be quite rare, and if it is all of your eggs, GET MORE CHICKENS! For worse case scenario to actually fully play out, it's often because someone tried to make a quick buck. I heard Gary Vaynerchuk tell a story about how a young man who was 19 years old came up to him and said, "Hey man, I lost $65,000 and now I have no money, what should I do?" Gary (from his description of the story, sadly I wasn't there) pauses for a moment and says, "What crazy cockamamie scam did you buy into trying to make a quick buck?"

And the young guy laughed and said, "How did you know?"

And Gary said, "Because that's the only way someone so young would lose so much money so quickly."

If we really think about that, how many risks have you

taken where every dollar you owned was on the table, at risk, ready to be lost with one toss of dice, so to speak? Or maybe literally.

Mr. Rudyard Kipling in his poem IF said,

"If you can make one heap of all your winnings

And risk it on one turn of pitch-and-toss,

And lose, and start again at your beginnings

And never breathe a word about your loss;"

I mean, people have been there!! It's happened! It can occur! I wouldn't personally advise in favor of gambling every single currency unit you can muster on a roll of dice, because the odds aren't in your favor. That's why gambling and investing in the stock market are different. If you take $100,000 and invest it into a well known, reputable company, versus putting it in on black on the roulette table and the ball hits red, what's going to happen? In gambling, the money is gone. Bye. See ya. Finished. Terminated. Over. Done. Wrecked.

But in the stock market, the stock could totally go down some without question but is it going to hit $0.00 overnight? Or in one day? A large, reputable company? Like BP (British Petroleum), or SalesForce, Amazon, Apple, JPMorgan? No. They will not go to zero overnight. I've actually never heard of an instance where in one swoop a stock goes from anything to just zero overnight. It at least takes days or weeks, depending of course on the price where you bought it. Anyway, that's another discussion for another time. That is the huge difference between investing in the stock market and gambling - the control of risk.

Many people will feel like all of their eggs are being risked if they only have one stream of income, their JOB (just over broke). This is because if you lose that job, there is no more money coming in. I'll tell you a fun story. I was spending time with a friend recently and we were chatting about his job, his future, and what impact he wants to have on the world.

He said, 'I would love to quit my job, but I don't have enough money saved up.'

And I said, 'Well, how much do you have saved?'

His reply? "About six months worth of bills in my savings account."

I was astounded! Six months! That's amazing! So, you're telling me, you could quit *right now* and *still* pay each bill you have for six months.

He smiled sheepishly, knowing where I was headed.

"And all of the money you have saved up is in your savings account?"

"No, I also have about $20,000 in my 401k," he said.

I challenged, "If you had to, how long would that cover the bills?"

"At least another six months."

"WOW! So you have an entire year of bills saved up?" I confirmed.

"Yeah, I guess I do. Huh, I never did the math."

"When are you going to give your two weeks' notice then?"

He laughed really hard and said, "Once I figure out exactly what I am going to do instead."

I said, "That's fair."

Why do I bring that up?

Without bringing too much theology into the picture or massive speculation about simulations, we are alive right now, and this is likely our one shot to consciously be alive. If you are doing something that is not fulfilling and exciting, change roles! Find alternate paths!

Let's make sure we understand a few key facts before moving forward:

- You can acquire more chickens to produce more eggs.

- Even if it's 'all of your eggs' in one basket, you can build certain devices to protect those eggs from breaking if you do accidentally drop the basket.

- You can build a really sturdy basket in case it is dropped. So, your eggs are fine. When you were in elementary school, did you have the science fair contest thing that required you to build a contraption that you placed an egg in, and then drop it from a high distance and see if your egg was protected? Yeah, I won that contest. Ever since then, I've had no fear of my eggs breaking.

Also realize, those who 'make it' financially in life usually placed copious amounts of their 'eggs' into one singular basket. Eggs in this situation could be time spent in a career field, time spent learning a craft, or currency placed in a safe investment vehicle. Mostly, it will boil down to the proper understanding and mastery of a specific subject, skill set, sector, or asset. Which, as we mentioned in a previous chapter, could be anything.

Debt is bad.

I love this one, simply because it's so poignant and succinct. It doesn't give us much information. This becomes a phrase that we all live by without much additional information.

Some debt can be bad, yes. The debt *most* people have is bad. Credit card debt can certainly and often times be bad, because the interest rates are so high. However, some debt is excellent! And this is what we must learn to have a proper relationship with money.

I'm actually going to continue my story from above. This gentleman later mentioned he would like to flip houses, but didn't have enough money. To which I asked, "How much money do you need to flip a house?"

And he said, "I'm not really sure, a hundred thousand dollars probably."

"A good guess for sure. It would certainly depend on the house. What I know for sure to be true is, you can buy a house with only a 20% down payment. You do not need to buy the entire house in cash. There are different ways to do it of course, but if you buy a $200,000 home to do a flip, you would only need $40,000 down. And then from there, you have the cost of hiring out labor, materials, holding costs, and utilities, along with other items to complete the flip, which could be another $30,000. These are just rough estimates. Totally spitballing here, but that would be, what, $70,000?"

He said, "Yep. Well, see, I don't have $70,000."

I countered, "You are close! You have $20,000 in savings and $20,000 in your 401k. That's $40,000. Do you have *any other money* anywhere else? Remember, it grows on trees?"

He smiled. "I mean, I have equity in my house."

"WHAT?! You have equity in your home? How much?"

"About $70,000," he replied.

Hold up. Let's first define equity. JUST in case, because why not. If one person learns something new from this following sentence, my mission is fulfilled.

Most commonly, equity means the difference between assets and liabilities. If a person owns a home worth $300,000 and they only owe $200,000 to the bank, that's $300,000 - $200,000 = $100,000 of equity. AKA money, currency, greenbacks and 'skrill'.

So, my friend owed about $230,000 on his home but fair market value is worth about $300,000.

Anyway, picking back up at the tail end of our conversation:

"DUDE!"

"Yeah, but I can't touch the equity in my home, what if I lose it?"

This is a great question! Very valid for him to ask.

What if he loses the equity in his home? Everyone is always told, 'never mess with the equity in your home.'

That is simply because large percentages of people do really stupid things with this money. They buy liabilities and not assets. People will buy boats, expensive cars, high-end jewelry, items that usually bring in very little return. We actually will be addressing this next.

The residual fears begin to take over, and money is just left sitting on the proverbial table. Money loves to work! That's one of its favorite things to do. You must love your money and let it do what it loves doing, which is going out and returning to you with friends.

Therefore, *learning* how to use a HELOC properly and profitably is something to embrace, rather than fear.

But a HELOC is expensive.

Ehhhh, not really. Sure, banks want to make money. Right now, towards the end of 2018, in the US, HELOC rates are around 4-6% depending on where you go. You can lock in a fixed rate HELOC and use this tool for so many possibilities.

Let's break down the numbers. If you pay 6% simple interest on a HELOC annually, that's $6,000 for every $100,000 borrowed. If you can make *more* than the $6,000 each year, it becomes a profitable endeavor.

The other exciting news? Loads of humans have equity in their home! This presents wonderful opportunities! Investing in real estate, businesses, franchises, or stocks all become a viable direction to walk in.

Aside from that, most countries have piles of debt, and almost every company has some form of debt. Debt fuels growth! Debt is extremely important, and if it's financed properly it can help surge performance.

Simply stated, there is no need to fear debt. The best debt is the kind that can be paid for easily while it generates more money and more growth. Embrace the ability to understand debt, to know how it works and how it's used. To get some wonderful information on this subject, go watch this YouTube video right now: *How the Economic Machine Works* by Ray Dalio. He discusses debt, credit, and how both are tied together and used to generate growth cycles along with recessive cycles. Solid video! Certainly worth checking out.

Who wants to be filthy rich?

Whoa! Wait just a few minutes. Why is getting rich, filthy? One of the first instances when I brought up the idea of this book in a public setting was while eating crab legs whilst sipping on a Pina Colada at Monty's Raw Bar in Miami, FL. It was a humble setting, eight or so excited clients were all chatting away and enjoying some appetizers. When I brought up the 'idea' about this book I asked, "What do you all think the hardest part of getting wealthy is?"

The first answer was from Joe. And he said in a very Bohemian way, "It all starts in your mind man. It's all about the thoughts in our brain and what we believe."

To which I replied "YES!!"

Then Joe went on to give an elaborate and in-depth discussion on his beliefs, his mental limitations and his thoughts. One of my takeaways was his feelings of disdain towards the term 'filthy rich.' He mentioned a couple of times how he didn't like this term and he didn't want to be viewed as a filthy person. And who does? This just happens to be yet another seemingly innocent mental barrier that will hold millions of people back from achieving financial riches.

Because very few, if any, want to be perceived as nasty, muddy, obscene, soiled, crummy, disheveled, slimy, unclean and unkempt. All synonyms for the term filthy.

I googled the origination of the phrase. This was really fun. One of the first things that popped up was "What's the meaning of the phrase 'Filthy rich?' Very rich, possibly having become so by unfair means."

I laughed at the word 'possibly.' Which word is stronger, possibly or probably? My answer is 'probably' means it is probable. A greater than 50/50 chance of happening. An example would be I will probably consume a chocolate milkshake by the end of the week. A moment of vulnerability here, that's 100% going to happen.

The reason I'm making a deal over this, it seems to me like someone was simply sour. 'Possibly becoming rich by unfair means.' What's unfair anyway? The entire sentence is dripping with subconscious belief that getting rich is not possible without cheating someone.

And then the article went on to say filthy rich "can't be explained without looking at the word lucre. From the 14th century lucre has meant money and is referred to as such by no less writers than Chaucer and John Wyclif. These references generally included a negative connotation and gave rise to the terms "foul lucre" and "filthy lucre," which have been in use since the 16th century. "Filthy lucre" appears first in print in 1526 in the works of William Tindale:

"Teachinge thinges which they ought not, because of filthy lucre."

Tindale was here using the term to mean dishonorable gain.

Following on the the term "filthy lucre," money became known by the slang term "the filthy," and it isn't a great leap from there to the rich being called the "filthy rich."

And there we have it, 500 years of a slow and trepidatious mind mold that began to alter the beliefs and thoughts of our ancestors. Maybe I'm being to dramatic? Or am I spot on? Either way, it's a real thing! The fear of becoming filthy rich is an unconscious blockade that impedes hundreds of millions of us on this Earth from obtaining our deepest financial desires.

I implore you to explore your thoughts and feelings on the term filthy rich. Is it possible or probable that becoming 'filthy' in the eyes of your friends or family is holding you back? Do you believe, somewhere in the deep caverns of your mind, this idea might be keeping you financially grounded? Or what about this very common belief and teaching?

Cars are Bad Investments

This is a fun one for me to attempt to tackle. I'm actually not really a car guy, but maybe it's a limiting belief I have. One thing I would challenge you to do is to still ask yourself this question, "How can I make this into an asset, rather than just a liability?" Feel free to use those words. It brings more validity to your brain. If you are about to buy something, anything, ask yourself how it can be used as an asset. "How can this make me money?"

If you are buying a car, boat, house, bed, coffee table, or TV set, ask the question, "How can this make me money?" Then, really think through it. If you cannot come up with one singular reason why or how something will make you money, do not buy it.

Here is an example:

A new bed. Why should anyone spend money on a new bed? A new bed means better sleep. Resting more soundly refreshes the *soul*. Sleep is good! If you are a human, you need sleep. That is a pretty basic fact. If you sleep better and get more rest, you are a better version of yourself, and likely, you will be able to make more money. You will work better, sell more effectively, think more clearly and sharply, remember more, and wake up ready to tackle the world!

This line of thinking can work with just about any purchase, and it gives you credence for your purchases. It helps you care more about *some* of your items and also helps you remove items. If you find certain items in your life that bring in very little value or actually cost you money, get rid of them.

Cars are certainly a depreciating asset, there's no argument there. But if you buy the right car at the right time, the deprecation has already occurred. Without getting into the discussion of what the future holds for transportation, it's obvious that humans need to get from point A to point B safely. I personally feel we have another 200 to 300 years before teleportation becomes a 'thing,' if ever. I know in major cities, humans can easily travel without the use of a personal vehicle. Their money is spent on Ubers, taxis, subways, trains, and other mass transit. Fact is, it will cost money to travel.

But if your car brings you more joy and happiness in life, and it's a peaceful environment where you enjoy serenity and it makes you feel better, it's a good investment. If the car runs well, is well maintained, clean, suitable and you enjoy it, swell job!

The issue is that the average American spends nine hours in their car a week (thanks to a random stat I just made up), but they hate their cars. They are messy trash heaps which barely run, tires are always flat, the engine barely cranks, the serpentine belt makes that awful sound, and it's just an energy suck.

It's super important to remember how powerful our subconscious mind is. What you tell it, what you believe, or what you were told to believe all starts at a young age. We have the ability to rewire our subconscious minds and reprogram our energies and thoughts. Henry Ford was quoted to say, "He who thinks he can and he who thinks he can't are both right."

At some point, my friends, the belief has to be there. The doubt has to be killed, the path has to be formed and walked upon. The more we carve out these paths in our minds, it becomes easier and easier to approach the next obstacle, hurdle, challenge and pathless Amazonian rainforest that lies before us.

Repeat to yourself each day that money does grow on trees. Repeat how much you love money. Repeat that it's okay to love money, to love growth, to be addicted to success! It's perfectly reasonable to help others grow and get rewarded for that! Repeat to yourself each day that it's our resourcefulness that will acquire what we seek, because the resources are always there!

If you treat money as an energy, as something that has actual feelings, you will notice your level of interaction with it will substantially transform!

We know that apples have seeds, yes? And when the apples fall onto the ground, bugs and other critters eat those apples, eventually spreading the seeds into different locations. All plants want to *grow, expand* and *reproduce*. Same as humans. This is the cycle of life. If an apple tree wants to grow, then so does your money!

Money wants to be loved, cared for, protected and it also wants to grow. It doesn't want to be spent on frivolous things. Money yearns to be spent on items, trips, vacations, journeys, memories, and experiences that make your life better!

When you begin to do this, you will make your brain happy. And any time your brain is happy, it will do its best to replicate that feeling by any means necessary. Rely on your brain. It will be your most powerful tool for growth, success, wealth, and prosperity!

Thank you for reading, and I truly hope your life will forever be impacted and enriched! :-)

Find me at:

Instagram
@jerremynewsome

Twitter
@newsomenuggets

Facebook
https://www.facebook.com/
jerremyalexandernewsome/

Youtube
https://www.youtube.com/c/
JerremyNewsomeEnrichesLives

www.jerremynewsome.com

www.treesaremoney.com

Find me also at:

www.reallifetrading.com

Instagram
@reallifetrading

Twitter
@reallifetrading

Made in the USA
Coppell, TX
14 October 2021

64074537R00090